W9-BJP-352

The Divine Dance

The Divine Dance

If the world is your stage,
who are you performing for?

by Shannon Kubiak

BARBOUR
PUBLISHING

© 2003 by Shannon Kubiak

ISBN 1-59310-021-3

Cover photo © Photonica

All rights reserved. No part of this publication may be reproduced or transmitted in any form or by any means without written permission of the publisher.

Unless otherwise noted, Scripture quotations are taken from the New American Standard Bible, © 1960, 1962, 1963, 1968, 1971, 1972, 1973, 1975, 1977, 1995 by the Lockman Foundation. Used by permission.

Scripture quotations marked KJV are taken from the King James Version of the Bible.

All Scripture quotations marked NKJV are taken from the New King James Version. Copyright © 1979, 1980, 1982 by Thomas Nelson, Inc. Used by permission. All rights reserved.

Published by Barbour Publishing, Inc., P.O. Box 719, Uhrichsville, Ohio 44683, www.barbourbooks.com

 Member of the
Evangelical Christian
Publishers Association

Printed in the United States of America.
5 4 3 2 1

To Mom, Dad, Darlin', and Papa—
thanks for being the loudest of my balcony people.
I love you guys!

And for my Lord and Savior Jesus Christ—
thanks for setting my heart to the rhythm of writing and
for giving me the chance to dance. I love You so much!

Foreword

All the fairy tales are true, you know.

There is a real Prince. He came from the vast kingdom of His Father with one purpose: to woo and win His long sought-after bride. One day, He will return to carry her away and they will be together forever.

Thousands of stories, movies, and songs tell this story. All of them have borrowed the theme from one book: the Bible.

Several years ago I was on a live radio interview where the host started by saying, "How can you call yourself a Christian and write 'romance' novels?" In that moment (after gulping mightily), I had a piercing thought.

"It's because when I was in high school I read a book that changed my life," I answered. "In the first few chapters everything falls apart and you think they're never going to get back together. About three-quarters of the way through the book, he moves heaven and earth to prove his love for her and still she won't come wholeheartedly to him. But finally—in the last chapter—he comes riding in on a white horse and takes her away to be his bride and live with him forever."

The radio host scoffed. "How could a book like that change your life? It sounds like a formula romance novel to me."

I grinned and said, "Really? That's funny—because I was

talking about the Bible. There's a white horse and everything."

The host froze. Radio listeners everywhere caught nothing but dead air.

"It's all true," I said plainly. "God is the Relentless Lover and we are His first love. He never gives up on us because He wants us back."

We cut to station break rather abruptly and the radio host looked at me through teary eyes. "You're right. I never saw it that way before."

For nearly two decades I have been sharing this truth with young women under the cover of novels. Forty of them, to be exact. When I read *The Divine Dance*, I couldn't stop smiling. Shannon has captured in this one book the essence of everything I've wanted to say to teens for so long. It's all here: truth, hope, gentle correction, and a brilliant spotlight on God, the Relentless Lover, who has been dearly longing to have this dance with you.

Robin Jones Gunn
Best-selling, award-winning author of the Christy Miller, Sierra Jensen, and Glenbrooke series, as well as the Sisterchicks novels

Contents

Setting the Stage

*I*n a busy, noisy world, a little girl walks onto a dark stage and begins to perform. She wears her pink princess costume with pride.

"Will you love me?" her actions ask. "Will you hold me; will you keep me close to your heart forever?"

The pain in her eyes screams at you. And with graceful pirouettes across the stage, she beckons you to choose her, to set her apart from the other performers, and to call her beloved. She has wounds buried so deeply beneath her costume that she has almost forgotten they are there. But the laughter of her audiences echoes through her mind as she thinks of all of the times she has tried and failed. All she has ever wanted is acceptance, but she has never found it—at least not for long.

Inside each of us is a desire to be loved, a desire to be chosen, and a desire to be called out of the crowd and loved for who we are. And seeking these desires, we all become performers, morphing ourselves into whatever role may earn us a place in the hearts of those around us. We constantly audition for affection, and once we have it, we feel we have attained perfection. We put all of our energy into our performances as we please our audiences however we can.

To become beautiful is the ogre's dream; to remain beautiful is the dream of the prom queen. But to be chosen is everyone's dream. What we fail to notice as we desperately dance is that One has never left His seat during our performance. Many audiences have come and gone, but this One, this Man, has sat there from day one and has never taken His eyes off of the little girl in the pink princess dress. His eyes answer the questions her eyes ask; His heart satisfies the needs of her heart. If only that little girl would take the time to notice, if she would stop focusing on herself and what she has to do to be beautiful to the

She has been missing the Divine Dance

because she has been too busy dancing for

men and princes to notice the King.

other audiences, she would see that she is already beautiful to this One. He has called her the beloved, and He is offering her an important role in His dance—the Divine Dance.

> *At the core of each one of us is the desire*
>
> *to be loved and accepted.*

She holds center stage in His heart. He has seen her at her best and her worst. He knows her flaws, but still He wants her. He wants to love her, to hold her, to keep her close to His heart forever. He has seen all of her costumes and sat through all of her performances, but He likes her best when she's not performing at all. He likes her best at the end of the day, when the other audiences are gone and she has taken off all of her masks. Whether she's smiling or crying, He loves her. And He wants to give her the world. But her concentration on her performances has kept her from seeing this answer to all her heart has ever wanted. God calls out to her, but she cannot hear Him. She is missing the fulfillment of her dreams and plans and the desires of her heart. Somewhere along the line she disregarded the invitation God sent because she was invited to another party put on by the world. But the world never told her she would be cast aside the moment she failed to mesmerize them.

That little girl is you. Each of us is a dancer; we dance our way through life, performing for others. We perform for our parents by getting good grades and cleaning our rooms. We perform for friends by wearing the right clothes and doing what they do. We perform for the guys we know by dressing to impress and putting our best flirt forward. We perform for teachers by passing their tests and knowing the right answers. We even perform for people we don't know. And by the time we've reached our teen years we have become artists.

> *You are unfulfilled because God*
>
> *did not create you to dance for this world.*
>
> *He intended for you to dance for Him.*
>
> *Dancing is a form of worship,*
>
> *and He wants you to worship Him.*

You don't believe me? Then why did you spend so long in front of the mirror when you got ready this morning? Because you wanted to make a certain statement when you walked out of the door. You wanted to say something about yourself without using any words. You wanted to perform. Maybe you don't use makeup. Perhaps you use sports or grades to perform instead. We are all performers, and we audition for a place in the hearts of everyone we meet.

You want to be beautiful to someone—anyone. That can get you into trouble, because there is a world out there that will lie to you. It will tell you whatever you want to hear to get what it wants from you. As a young Christian girl, you have a lot to offer. You possess authenticity, and that's a rhythm the world can never dance to. At best, the world offers poor imitations of everything you've ever wanted.

So why, then, do you dance so hard on its stage? Why do you try so hard to please the crowd? And why are you always unfulfilled? You dance because you want to be noticed, and you try so hard because everyone else wants to be noticed, too.

He has gifted you exclusively for this purpose. He has wrapped you in the package that is your personality and your body so you can play a certain role. Long ago He wrote a script, and He wrote a role for you that's all your own, and only *you* can play it. Without you, the story cannot continue as it was originally intended. Without you, lesser methods have to be chosen, and somewhere the CD in God's divine CD player skips a beat. "Someone is not dancing like she should," it seems to say. You cannot dance for God the way you have been dancing. God will not share His glory. But He will share His love, and that is what this dance is all about.

When you get up on that stage and seek your own glory or seek the world's applause, you break God's heart. Yeah, you are dancing, but it's all to no avail. You're missing the story. You're missing the dance. Deep inside you are dissatisfied, and even if nobody else knows it, God does. He wants to change that; He wants to give you the riches of His kingdom.

> *God designed you to glorify Himself.*
>
> *He designed the Divine Dance so others may*
>
> *see your life and want to glorify Him, too.*

He wants you to dance for Him, but it will cost you—although not as much as you think. You only have to give up the world, and the riches of heaven will be yours. Take off the vanity-stained leotard the world has given you and slip on God's grace. He wants to clothe you in righteousness and set you apart. In the end, that's a far better deal than working really hard for seven seconds in the spotlight and a loveless reality.

Today you can have the performance of a lifetime, and I hope you don't pass it up. You can watch from the sidelines, but it won't do you any good.

You can dance your hardest for this world, but when you wind up with a trophy made out of fool's gold, you won't be very happy.

These are pivotal times in your life. The choices you make from here on out will define who you are. The costumes you wear will label you. Adulthood is just around the corner now; maybe you've found it already. Soon enough, nobody will make choices for you anymore, and as nice as it sounds, a lot of responsibility comes with that. So practice making wise decisions right now. Dance for the One who deserves to be worshiped. Dance for the One who desires to be worshiped. And dance for Him alone.

You were born with feet that dance

and a heart that hears rhythm,

so you have to dance for someone.

You can't help yourself.

No matter your music or your style, dance unto the Lord. Not only will you be changed, but you will change others with your song.

Chapter 1

Auditioning for a Role in the Story: Dancing for the World

We all start dancing for other people shortly after we learn how to walk. Even when we're just infants and children, we figure out what will make our families smile, so we do *this*. We learn what makes them angry, and we don't do *that*. Haven't you ever been to an elementary school play and seen the little boy in the back row picking his nose? Do you think maybe he's picking it because he wants a reaction? Suddenly all eyes are off of the little girl with the solo, and giggles are muffled as fingers point to the child who's digging for gold. Most of the time he smiles, knowing that now the audience is watching him.

Don't worry, the theme of this book runs far deeper than "Stop picking your nose." But I do think that message carries a lot of weight. Think about how many times you did something, big or small, just to be noticed this past week. Maybe you wore a certain outfit; maybe you spoke loud enough for someone not in your direct conversation to overhear what you were saying. Maybe you developed an attitude because you weren't getting your way. I have no idea what your answer is, but I do know one thing: Girls are masters at the art of seeking attention. I spent two years of my life in a dorm building with nearly four hundred girls. I know a lot of the secrets that we have all become so good at hiding.

The concept of the Divine Dance is something God began to open my eyes to during my first year at college. I had seen evidences of it during high school and while working in junior high and high school ministry, but not until college did I realize just how hard each of us works to please our audiences. During my first semester at a Christian university, I began to see how many girls suffered from severe eating disorders or had other serious image issues. While living in a dorm with several hundred other young women, I saw how the concept of performance consumes our lives.

We stand for hours in front of the mirror putting on makeup, trying on clothes, and curling our hair so we look just right. But all it takes to undo all of our hard work is for one person to tell us that we don't look good. Sometimes it doesn't even take that much. Our images of ourselves come from the images others have of us.

If they smile, we beam. If they chuckle, we laugh. If they hum, we sing. If they frown, we cry. At a recent Bible study, my friend Amy quoted one of her professors:

"I am not who you think I am. I am not who I think I am. I am who I think you think I am," Dr. Shelly Cunningham shared.

Let that sink in. We are who we think others think we are—when masks and costumes enter the story.

We are like dancers. We dance for family, friends, teachers, guys, and sometimes even ourselves. We dance for attention, and we dance for applause. But somewhere in the midst of all the noise, we forget that we were made to dance for God. The world offers us popularity, and our eyes grow big with visions of fame. The world offers us money, and cash registers ring in our minds at the idea of what we can buy. The world offers us acceptance, and we camouflage ourselves to fit in. The world offers us romance, and our hearts ache with the idea of love. We want it all.

> *We delight in the positive responses*
>
> *of our audiences.*

Every girl wishes she could be the prettiest or the smartest, the most athletic or the best dressed. Every girl wants to stand out, and so she dances. She does a little ballet, some jazz, a little tap, a bit of hip-hop, and, of course, the salsa. And thus the performance begins.

We might as well walk around holding up signs that read, "Pick me, pick me." Because that's what we are doing. We are begging to be chosen, pleading to be loved. And we morph ourselves into whatever characters can attain these things. In these auditions our masks become our faces, and we lose ourselves. We lose the individuality that God has given us, and we lose sight of God Himself.

We watch all of these Hollywood movies, and we tell ourselves that is how life is. Two people meet, they fall in love, and with the world at their disposal, they live happily ever after. We see beauty as something developed by a quick fifteen minutes in a tanning bed—not something developed internally over a lifetime. We see it, we want it, and we seek it. Often, we are not willing to wait. The world whispers to us, telling us we can be whatever we want and have all of these things that blind our eyes. So we dance, and we dance, and we dance—all for an empty happiness. At the end of the audition we are cast aside, and someone else gets the role that we thought was so truly us, and we are devastated.

≋ ≋ ≋

Back before time began, God developed a plan. He would

create us, and we would worship Him. Psalm 149:3 tells us, "Let them praise His name with dancing."

When we dance for this world and seek our own glory, we break the number one commandment. "Thou shalt have no other gods before me" (Exodus 20:3 KJV). We have made ourselves and our audiences our idols. No wonder we find no satisfaction. How can God bless us if we are living in sin by putting ourselves and our audiences before Him?

> *Dancing is a form of worship,*
>
> *and when we dance for*
>
> *others we become idolaters.*

So how do we stop ourselves from dancing for other audiences? First of all we need to take a look at Romans 12:2, "And do not be conformed to this world, but be transformed by the renewing of your mind, so that you may prove what the will of God is, that which is good and acceptable and perfect." We need to change our way of thinking. We need to go back to the basics and find out what this Divine Dance is all about.

Most of us avoid the Divine Dance because we are afraid it will cost us our comfort, our friends, our status, and our masks.

Each of us has different kinds of masks, but they all give us something to hide behind. Maybe your mask is excelling in school, perhaps it is an incredible athletic ability, maybe it is a beauty-queen-type status of popularity, or perhaps it's being the class clown. Our masks are usually whatever we use as our greatest defense mechanisms—to hide the real selves we think others won't like.

> *We are afraid to dance without our masks*
>
> *because they give us a false sense of security.*

We think that we will never amount to anything, because the Divine Dance is not as popular or well known in our society. It is not showy enough, and there's not enough glitter for the world. We throw God's Script in the reject pile because we think it has nothing to offer. We're right about there not being any glitter, but we overlook the fact that there is gold. We throw out authenticity for a cheap imitation; then we wonder why we are unfulfilled. We were made for the real thing. Each one of us is royalty. That is why each one of us so desperately desires to get the acclaim due a princess.

You have been auditioning for the lead role in other plays when God has already cast you in the Divine Dance, which is a much greater story. He has given you a role that no other can play, and production has been at a standstill in your absence. Your life isn't playing out the way God designed it to if you are dancing for other audiences. What you have forgotten is that as a Christian you get to be different—a good "different." It's a stand-out-and-make-the-world-take-notice different.

≈ ≈ ≈

When it comes to seeking God's will for our lives, many of us wonder, *Just what is the good, acceptable, and perfect will of God?* It's the story of the potter and the clay. "But the vessel that he was making of clay was spoiled in the hand of the potter; so he remade it into another vessel, as it pleased the potter to make," Jeremiah 18:4 says. God thinks you're beautiful, but He wants you to be radiant. God made you bright, and He wants you to shine.

We are princesses;

we just haven't been living that way.

We have forgotten our role.

So He must strip you of your glitter; He must tear you away from your fans, and He must take you into a quiet practice studio and teach you all over again how to truly dance. He must groom you for your role on the world's stage. He must teach you to give the glory to Him and to stop striving for the world's approval.

> *God wants to use you in the world for His glory, but first He must take the world out of you.*

At first you may be lonely—the quiet blackness of a studio may seem dim in comparison to the bright stages the world gave you. But Romans 12:1–2 tells us to not be conformed (shaped, molded) into the image of this world but to renew our minds so that we can find God's perfect will. Renewing your mind means stepping off of the stage for a moment. It means learning to dance all over again, because we have to learn to dance in a different way.

In God's studio, you will find that the answers do not lie within you, and you cannot do it all. You will discover that true beauty is in the dancer's heart, not in her costume. You do not need to stand apart from everyone else, and you will never need to ask God to pick you. You have already been chosen. You already hold center stage in His heart. So stop auditioning and dance.

Before a dancer ever performs, she must endure grueling hours of training. She must listen to the same song hundreds of times to learn to match her steps to the rhythm and predict every pause. She must learn each step separately before she can blend them together. She will probably sweat and cry a few times before she ever reaches the stage.

And so it is with the Divine Dance. Before you are ever ready to dance for the Lord with the world watching, you must dance for the Lord's eyes alone.

As you stand in the middle of God's classroom and wait for the music to start, He gives you only one command: "Worship Me." He leaves you the freedom to let your creative juices flow. Don't be afraid to be bold; God made you. You don't need to impress Him, because He knows your heart. But He also knows your capabilities, so dance with all your might. As you dance from your soul for the God who created you, you will be consumed with worship.

One who dances for the kingdom reflects

the kingdom in all of her steps.

At last your heart will begin to beat with God's heart. You will hear a song written just for you, and you will dance the dance you have wanted to dance your whole life. No masks, no auditions, no audience but One. A weight will be lifted from your shoulders, because there is no pressure in God's practice studio. He is the ever patient Teacher. With each graceful movement you take toward God, you will find the dance becomes easier. Spending time with your Coach by reading God's Word before your day begins will help you drown out the voices of temptation you will hear throughout your day. Taking a few steps back from friends who have a negative influence on you will give you the freedom to move as God pleases. Using your own gifts to serve God will give you a sense of purpose.

These changes won't always be easy or natural to make. Eventually, you may find yourself auditioning once again. You will want to show the world all of the wonderful things you have learned, but people will see no difference. Every time you dance for the world, you always look the same. You look like a glory hound. You have a big neon sign strapped to your head that reads, "Look at me! I am a superstar." And the lessons you learned in the classroom slip away. You can never dance the Divine Dance *for* the world, although someday you may be able to dance it *in front of* them. Although you will forever remain a student of the Divine Dance, you will one day move from studio to stage where the whole world will see you dance. But you must know the steps before you ever step onto the stage. They are steps of obedience, humility, grace, and love.

If you truly take the time to understand who God is and allow Him to be glorified in every stage of your life, you will find that dancing is no longer a burden, and you will experience it as the joy it was created to be.

> *Dancing for God connects us to Him*
>
> *in a way nothing else really can.*

It is a process that takes time, and you need not get discouraged when your best efforts fail—just try again.

~ ~ ~

Back in God's studio, you see no hint of frustration on His face, only love. He patiently sits in the corner and says, "Worship Me." And He watches as you look at yourself in the mirror and dance with all your might.

Man, I look good, you think. And God shakes His head, knowing that you just don't get it. The music stops and you keep dancing, absorbed in yourself. God clears His throat, and you stop, waiting to be praised.

"Let's start over again," God says. Yet you don't understand. You just danced the performance of a lifetime.

"Worship Me," God says, and you are confused. You ask, "Isn't that what I was just doing?" Again God shakes His head.

Frustrated, you put your head in your hands and scream. Sometimes you wish you were back on the world's stage, where your high jumps and graceful twirls delighted your audience. But God is somewhat unimpressed with all of that. Then the door opens. God has called in the Master of the Divine Dance to show you what you haven't been able to see. Jesus steps into the room, and the darkness fades into light.

Your role is to dance in such a way that others take notice and want to dance like you, too. You are to worship God so boldly that the whole world will want to worship Him. It's not about high jumps. It's not about self-glory. It's not even about you. It's not about the dancer; it's about the dance. It's about the story that God has written so the world might know Him.

And for the first time ever, you realize the difference. The world dances with pride; those who are divine dance with humility. So you shake the glitter from your hair and ask God if you can try again. He smiles as He starts the song. As you listen to the words, you think of all of the auditions you wasted your time on.

Your eyes well up with tears, and your heart breaks. You want to master the Divine Dance for the first time ever—not because you want the world to notice you, but because you want them to notice God. As you are thinking about this, you realize you are dancing. When you catch a glimpse of yourself in the mirror, you are amazed. You don't even look like the same girl. There is a purity about you now, a freshness the world doesn't have. And you thank God for the privilege of being a part of the story.

The music starts and He begins to dance.

And as you watch Him, you hear the

words to the music for the first time:

" 'For even the Son of Man did not come

to be served, but to serve,

and to give His life a ransom for many' "

(MARK 10:45).

That's it. That's the difference.

This dance is not about you.

This dance, this Divine Dance,

is God's way of drawing people to Himself.

This type of transformation often occurs after a dancer has had her heart broken. Perhaps you are in a place where you feel as if God's light will never shine again. Maybe you fear that letting this type of transformation occur in your life will cause you to get booed off of the stage, and you will lose the audience and reputation you have worked so hard to gain. True, dancing for God will change you so entirely that some of your old friends may not recognize you, but that is the beauty of brokenness.

He has not taken you off of the world's stage forever—just long enough for you to learn whom you were designed to dance for.

When we no longer know who we are and we have come to a place where we can drown out all that the world is saying, then we can hear God's gentle voice as He whispers in our ears and tells us who we are.

❧ ❧ ❧

Matthew 16:26 says, " 'For what will it profit a man if he gains the whole world and forfeits his soul?' " The answer is nothing. That is why God has called you off the stage and into His studio. You weren't necessarily dancing in the wrong place; you were just dancing the wrong dance. Perhaps you were dancing with the wrong people. Those who dance for the world, and spend their lives in and out of auditions, lose their souls. But God loved you too much to let that happen to you. So God interrupted your story, because He saw past the facade.

God looks deep into your heart and sees the music that moves you. He sees what you haven't been able to see. He sees what you are capable of doing. Just give Him some time, and be patient with yourself. You are still human. The world will miss you eventually, and they will want you back. They will invite you to audition for them again. This time, you will have a choice to make. Will you choose the well-lit stage and the costume with the sparkling glitter? Or will you turn your back on the stage and go back into the small practice studio to learn more about the dance God has for you?

If you said you'd choose the quiet studio, I'm glad. I chose it long ago and haven't had any regrets. And I'm still learning. Dances can be complicated. Some people dance a one-step routine; others dance a two-step dance, but not God. He dances a ten-step. And that's the dance He wants to teach us. This dance isn't easy to learn, and its complex nature means it will encompass every area of your life. It will affect not only your own growth and development but also your relationships with others. Elisabeth Elliot once said, "The fact that I am a woman does not make me a different kind of Christian, but the fact that I am a Christian makes me a different kind of woman."

So it is with us. The fact that we are dancers does not change our Christianity, but our Christianity should change how we dance.

The Divine Dance was meant to be lived out not only on the stage but also in friendships with Christians and non-Christians alike; in dating (or a lack of dating) relationships, in your relationships with your family, and, most importantly, in your relationship with God. Even if you have wandered away and are just now finding your way back to the stage—or if you are finding your way to the stage for the first time—you can live the Divine Dance with diligence and dedication.

You cannot dance for God with the world in your pocket.

So if I can offer you a piece of advice as you lace up your dancing shoes, let it be this: *Dance unashamed.* Rise up and shout that you are the beloved of God and that you are here to proclaim His name. Don't be quiet about it, and don't be timid. Praise His name with dancing. Give Him all the glory, and enjoy the performance—God will certainly enjoy it! As you dance, you will face hard times and tough sessions, but have fun. Let the music flow through you. Then, when you are ready, God will open the doors and lead you to the stage, where the world will be able to watch. What they see will amaze them, just as it amazed you when you caught your first glimpse of yourself dancing the Divine Dance.

The woman who dances only for God will be different. She will be unlike anything the world has ever seen. She will be bold and daring, gentle and caring—all at the same time. She will be you, but she will be more than you. She will be God in you—for the entire world to see. Enjoy the quiet time alone in the studio with God as you meditate on His Word and memorize His steps.

Get ready to live the life that you were truly meant to live, because God has been waiting for this moment ever since He gave you feet. Let the world fade into the background and dance for God alone.

Chapter 2

The Rhythm of Your Heart: Dancing to Your Own Music

Although every dancer wants to stand out, none of them wants to be different. The words "Well, she's just different" have a negative connotation. Nobody wants to invite other people's judgment and ridicule. Everybody wants to be a star, so we all force ourselves into the mold of what we think a star should be.

We might find ourselves like the contestants on the popular reality TV hit *American Idol*. We perform our best while on stage, begging the judges and the audience for votes, but we leave defeated when the brutal Simon Cowells of the world tell us that we do not "have what it takes." I cannot even watch that show because it is too painful to hear such criticism—even though he isn't even talking to me! Competitions for popularity often cause us to leave our originality at the door in order to avoid criticism.

So instead of a thousand stars being born to dance for God on the world's stage, too many times one star starts to shine. Then, suddenly, all of the others become her clone. Every group has one girl whom everyone else secretly longs to be like or pretends to be. Those secret longings have a way of creeping out of our closets and affecting our lives and relationships. If the girl everyone wants to be says something is cool, it is. She sets the standard. Yet all of her followers defeat their own purposes. They spend their lives trying to stand close enough to that one person so that her glow reflects onto them. We aren't meant to mirror others; we are supposed to shine our own original lights. We're to stand in our own spotlights on God's stage—not try to push our way into someone else's spotlight. Trying to steal or share someone else's glory won't give us the break we want, but dropping the facade and baring our hearts will bring us success.

Don't be afraid of who you really are deep down inside— don't suppress your deepest dreams and desires just to please or be like someone else. You have a dream in your heart because God put it there. And He placed it there with a purpose in mind. You've just got to find His reason. But as you look for the purpose, you cannot be afraid to be real.

꙳ ꙳ ꙳

I cringe every time I think of my first semester in college. I was so caught up in performing and trying to please those around me that I didn't even know who I was anymore. I bought clothes I didn't even like because I thought they would bring me attention and make me popular. I also hung out with people I had nothing in common with because they were a little older and could show me the way I was "supposed" to live. I was at a Christian college, and I still almost forgot that I was a daughter of God with individual gifts and abilities with which to worship Him—because I was afraid of being real. I was afraid of what being real could mean for my reputation.

Being real hurts because it makes us vulnerable. When we bare our souls, our hearts are open targets for attack. But we usually can't touch another heart until we open our own hearts. When I returned to college for my second year, I found my niche. I made friendships that will last a lifetime because I stopped trying to fit in and I just let myself be me.

> *God did not give you a face that reflects His glory so you can cover it up with a mask.*

God did not hide His heart from the world, and neither should you.

Nobody knows about unveiling our hearts better than King David. He penned the vulnerable words of Psalm 139:23–24, "Search me, O God, and know my heart; try me and know my anxious thoughts; and see if there be any hurtful way in me, and lead me in the everlasting way." And he stripped off his mask and danced before the Lord. Second Samuel 6:14 says, "And David was dancing before the LORD with all his might, and David was wearing a linen ephod." He was dancing for the Lord wearing only his undergarment. You can't get more vulnerable than that!

I don't encourage you to go streaking down the street in your pajamas, but I do encourage you to drop your mask and be yourself. Give God His rightful place in your life, and stop trying to create your own image and design your own destiny. You'll learn a lot more about God and His plan for your life that way.

After all, Psalm 100:3 says, "Know that the LORD Himself is God; it is He who has made us, and not we ourselves." You cannot write your own story, and you cannot control how God writes it, but you can count on the fact that the end of the story will make all of the other chapters worth it.

Dancing to the rhythm of your own heart is not always easy to do. Those who are wearing masks will mock and ridicule you because your authenticity makes them look fake—because they are. Those who wear masks yearn for liberation, no matter what they say. Yet fear holds them back from taking off their masks and being themselves, so they will look at you with disdain because of the freedom you are experiencing. This is what David's wife did. When we read about David dancing in Second Samuel, verse 16 tells us that Michal looked out of her window and saw David dancing, and she "despised him in her heart." She let David know it, too, but her opinions didn't stop him (verses 20–22). At that moment He was dancing for God alone.

Perhaps that was why God had made him king. But as David's life went on, he eventually stopped dancing for God and started dancing for his own pleasure. His mistakes led to deadly consequences, as they do for all of God's children. If God has called you to dance for Him, He will never let you get away with dancing for another.

> *Your heart is too valuable for God to share it*
>
> *with anyone or anything else.*

God's purposes are not always obvious. When David was a youth and Samuel anointed him as the next king, David probably didn't understand the magnitude of that. David was just a teenager when God promised him that he would one day be king. But several years and many trials passed before God let David wear his crown. No, God's purposes are not always obvious, and they aren't always immediate. Sometimes we even stumble into our callings by accident.

Each life is its own story, and each of us fights to write our story our own way. But God's hand is stronger, and His purposes are higher. He will take you down long and winding roads if that is what He needs to do to prepare you for your purpose. High school and college can seem especially hard as we get closer to graduation. The pressure mounts, and we are supposed to know exactly what we want to do with the rest of our lives. Teachers, parents, and people we don't even know start asking questions like "What do you want to do with your life?" And we can often feel as if someone has strapped a boulder to our backs.

When the curtain goes down on high school,

He will teach you the first steps of the

dance of college. When the curtain goes

down on college, He will teach you the

first steps in the dance of a career.

Whatever happened to youth being the best and most carefree time in our lives? As a young Christian you pray for guidance, but there is only silence. You strain to hear the music for the Divine Dance, but it's so faint you cannot seem to make out the tune. God is a God of seasons. He loves to watch the changing of the leaves, the falling of the snow, and the new growth that comes in the spring. He is also there in the seasons of your life.

> *God likes to use somewhat indirect routes*
>
> *to take us to where He wants us to be—*
>
> *at times He may teach us steps that don't*
>
> *seem to fit with the choreography He's*
>
> *already been teaching us. We don't always*
>
> *realize our gifts and our passions right away;*
>
> *sometimes they are unmasked through the*
>
> *events of our lives, through steps that*
>
> *don't seem to fit.*

And when the time is right, He'll teach you the next dance, and the next, and so on. He will teach you the dance you need to know when you are twenty, but don't worry about it when you are just eighteen.

One of the secrets of the Divine Dance is that God will not just start the music and leave the room. Nor is He predictable. He likes to change things every now and then. Just when you have mastered one song, He puts on another. The purpose of the dance is always the same, but the steps are often changed.

෨ ෨ ෨

The key to finding God's purpose and His song for you is twofold: Get to know God, and find out what you truly love. When I was in elementary school, I loved to perform. I would act; I would sing; I would do anything for an audience. And when I wasn't performing, I was pretending to do so. I used to go into my room by myself and turn on the radio. I would stand center stage and flash a huge smile to my bed, as if it were my audience. When the music started, I came to life. When I was through, I always imagined a thunderous applause. Unfortunately, I was never a good dancer. In fact, the only place I usually danced was in my room behind closed doors.

It's hard to have stage fright when

you have no audience.

One year of dancing lessons was enough to show me that I didn't have what it takes to be a great performer. But perhaps God gave me that passion for a higher purpose. After all, the analogy of dancing has spoken volumes into my spiritual life. Perhaps He has given you your passions for a higher purpose, as well.

But that is why it is so important to know God well. We tend to forget that God already has all of the answers—although we're still trying to figure them out. " 'Ask, and it will be given to you; seek, and you will find; knock, and it will be opened to you. For everyone who asks receives, and he who seeks finds, and to him who knocks it will be opened,' " Matthew 7:7–8 says. So ask God how your passions fit into His plans, and listen for the answers. We can hear His voice giving us the answers as we read His Word, sit in stillness before Him, listen to the messages at church, and seek counsel from godly men and women in our lives.

Many times God will teach us steps that will change us, because each of us has a drive that fights against our passion for God. These drives are unbridled or undisciplined passions, and they are what drove us to dance on the world's stage in the first place. Even when we try to leave them behind, they remain imbedded in who we are.

Things like a competitive nature or a jealous spirit can be considered unbridled passions. And the unbridled passion for affection causes many to start dancing for the world. Don't let your gifts or your passions go wild. Give them to God, and let Him help you develop and train your natural passion. Think about how many Christians started in bands or other Christian careers, musical or not, wanting to make an impact for God, only to lose sight of that goal when presented with opportunities of fame and fortune. Their original passion to serve God and affect the world got lost.

> *The things you are passionate about are usually an obvious clue to help you discern God's will. Figuring out how He wants you to use those passions can get kind of tricky.*

Sometimes our very desire for success can war against our passion for God. When we get out there on the world's stage, we need to keep reminding ourselves that our purpose is to tell God's story and not our own.

≈ ≈ ≈

In God's studio we can surrender our own unbridled passions and watch them transform into a rhythm that only God can create. So in a world that is telling you to find yourself, you need to find God first. As He teaches you to dance, He will weave your passions into His plan. He may have to tweak a few of them, but ultimately those passions are from Him—they just need to be shaped according to His plan. Remember that His plans may take longer to unfold, but they are always bigger and better in the end than anything we can imagine or do ourselves.

The song God has given you for this time in your life may be more valuable than you think. People are watching—especially if you've left the world's ways. They may only be watching for a slipped step or a missed beat, but they are watching. And they will notice the difference. Your story may speak volumes into the lives of people you didn't even know existed. When your heart is tuned to God's song, He will put you in the right place at the right time to use you for His glory. The catch is that you may not always get to see the results. So dancing like we're going to make a difference for God involves having faith that God knows the results.

For instance, during my sophomore year of high school I invited an older, good-looking boy to church camp. My friends condemned me, saying I had the wrong motives. But I was certain I had heard God's voice instructing me to invite Eric to camp. He came, we had fun, and Eric got saved. Time passed, he graduated, and I never heard from him again. . . until one summer at a local Bible college.

Eric stood to give his testimony in a class my mom's friend

taught. He said the greatest gift he had ever received was the gift of salvation, and that he got saved because a girl in high school had invited him to camp. The teacher asked who the girl was, and he said my name, smiling, not realizing that she knew me. Although I had moved away and gone to college, God still let me hear of this victory. Perhaps He let me hear about it to encourage me to keep dancing for the victories I would never see or hear about. There have been others like Eric in my life, and not all of those stories have such encouraging endings, yet this is where faith comes into practice. I knew I was hearing God and I listened, but at times I had to plug my ears against my friends' judgmental words. So what if I thought Eric was cute? Why shouldn't cute boys be invited to heaven? Don't misunderstand me—we have no excuse to flirt with the world. Dating unsaved guys will not get them to heaven, but inviting them to camp or church might. God clearly tells us that being unequally yoked is wrong and isn't in His plan. So in situations like that, you need to listen closely to God and be mindful not to take even one step in the wrong direction.

But I may have never known the difference that my dancing made in one boy's life if God hadn't let me catch a glimpse of His unfolding plan. When you get busy dancing for God alone, you forget about the other eyes that may be watching. Most of the time you're not aware of your full impact. But the world is watching. The people of the world may even be imitating you, and they may change their lives (and their dance), as well.

Life is one big moment made up of many tiny moments, and those tiny moments truly do matter most. Even just the expression on your face may speak to the souls of those who are watching you dance. Your smile and the light in your eyes may be enough for them to take notice.

> *You will be able to move mountains if you can move people, and you can move people if you know how to touch their hearts.*

If you consider all of the events of your life, the trials and the triumphs all form one story. The point of the story is redemption, and the underlying theme is love. If you can relate your story to other people's stories, even indirectly, you will change their stories by becoming a part of their lives. Some of my greatest friends and I bonded over similar hardships or heartaches we suffered. If you have ever been the new girl in school, then you know just how hard it is for the girl who just transferred to your school. Invite her to lunch—it may make more of a difference in her life (and yours) than you can ever imagine.

My friend Rebecca and I laugh about how we met. It was our first night living in our dorm building as freshmen in college. I went into the communal bathroom on our hall to wash my face, and I heard someone crying. When Rebecca emerged from the stall, I asked her if she was okay. She told me that she had just started her period and didn't have any feminine hygiene products. So I went back to my room and raided my own supply for her. As a result, I made a friend who, to this day, is one of my greatest friends. (That is, if she is still my friend after she finds out I told that story!) She appeared in a moment when I wasn't looking to meet a friend, and many times since then Rebecca has looked out for my needs as I looked out for hers that night.

⌐ ⌐ ⌐

As you dance, let your sensitivities make you sensitive to others. Let your passions be insights into the dreams of those around you. Meet them on their level. Find out what they are about. Think of all of the people who have touched your life and don't even know it. Your name is probably on the lists of a surprising number of people. Of course, they may recall your name for either positive or negative reasons. Is your name there because you danced into their hearts or because you danced on them?

Often, as we try to find our role in God's story, unfortunately we diminish someone else's role. It's that old glory-hound mentality again. A good dancer is always aware of the others on the stage. She leaves them the room they need to dance, and she gives them room to make mistakes.

Finding your own rhythm isn't about getting your audience to like you. It's about forgetting the audience and watching Jesus' feet as He trains you to dance the Divine Dance. It's not about never making a mistake. It's about taking off your masks and refusing to hide anymore. It's about dancing with the passions that are in you and letting the world see that God cares.

Take these three situations, for example:

- If you love art, paint in such a way that God's glory is revealed. Show the world that God cares about art school, scholarships, and providing all of the supplies. Paint for His glory, and the world will see the difference.

- If you love sports, give God the glory for the goal you scored, or the base you stole, or the MVP award you received. Dance with integrity and passion.

- If you are a musician, keep your lyrics positive and uplifting whether you perform for Christian audiences, secular groups, or both. Show the world that music is so powerful that it can stir both God's heart and people's hearts simultaneously.

If you can stand before your audience and tell them (or better yet, show them) that God placed your passion within your heart, then they may in turn see and acknowledge that He also put their passions in their hearts.

At times you will mess up; your dance will not be flawless. But God does not expect you to be perfect. He offers forgiveness to all who will accept it; your mistakes are part of this dance, too. After all, our mistakes are why we need a Savior. Believe it or not, you can even use your mistakes to tell about the Divine Dance. If your mistakes draw you to God, the mistakes of others may draw them to Him, too.

Whatever you do, don't give up. One of my roommates put a sign up in our living room that read, "Don't quit!" It is amazing the impact those two words can have on tough days. There are moments when the key to the Divine Dance is simply surviving until the next act.

⤞ ⤞ ⤞

Your rhythm is unique, and it is special, and when you blend it with others' choreography, the whole performance will be amazing. You never know the difference your dance may make in someone else's life. We may find many unexpected people in heaven who will be there because someone took the chance and took the time to show them how to dance.

Lead by example.

Dance with whatever gifts God has given you, and dance with all of those around you—don't try to make each dance a solo performance. And don't focus on the other dancers. Your job is to keep up the steps God is calling you to perform. As you dance and do your part, God will do His part, as well. He'll pull the heartstrings of all of those who are watching. And He'll bring your dance to their minds long after you have left the stages of their lives, because your dance is His dance, and He gifted you for this time and this place.

> *Saving souls is not up to you but dancing the Divine Dance is. Do your part; God will do His.*

And when tomorrow comes, and the scenery changes, you will find you are ready to learn the next number on the next stage of your life. Give God time to let His plans unfold. Don't worry about the next step. Take advantage of today and what you know. Dance right here with what you have, and God will make sure that you make it to wherever you need to be. And when you hear a pause in the Divine Dance, and you can't quite make out the tune, sit at your Teacher's feet and listen for what's next. According to Luke 19:17, those who are faithful in the small things will be trusted in the big things. Little by little, step by step, as you dance, let your life make a difference to others.

Never be discouraged if you only receive small rewards. Even if you touch only one life with your dance, you have still done your part. If one more dancer joins God's dance because of you, then you have made more of a difference than you could have ever hoped for. Not only have you touched one life, but you have also touched all of the lives touched by that other person. Stop looking at your audience as a mass surrounding you, and start looking at members of the audience as individuals within your reach. God brought them into your life for a reason. The Divine Dance may be about God, but it was designed to touch the hearts of those in your audience. And back before time began, God intended to touch them through you.

Chapter 3

The Importance of the Background Dancers: Dancing with a Difference

*L*ife is full of an interesting cast of characters. Since we are always on the stage of our own lives, and never in the audience, I think we fail to realize just how much of an impact the background dancers have on our performance and on our lives.

In high school and college, we really begin to transition into who we will be as adults, and we start spending less time with our families and more time with our friends. In fact, during college you may even start living with your friends. That is why it is so important to find like-minded friends. Having friends who are dancing the Divine Dance with you will vitally affect whether or not you will keep dancing for God. Having unsaved friends isn't a sin, but you need to be guarded in those friendships because they are more likely to lead you into sin.

When I remember my first few days of college, there are a few things I see more clearly now. In college, everywhere you turn people are performing to make friends. People in polished costumes with prepared speeches pop out at every corner asking you your name, where you are from, and what you do for fun. Girls start forming their "forever friendships" and their "families away from home" before classes even start.

You know the old saying "Birds of a feather flock together"? It never ceases to amaze me how people tend to find kindred spirits in only a few minutes. The art majors found the other art majors, and together they danced to the rhythm of their passion. The surfer girls found other surfer girls—and surfer boys—in a matter of minutes, and so on and so forth.

My first year away at school was especially hard because all I did was perform for other people. I was trying to find myself and change myself so I could be just like everyone around me. I came home for the summer hating college and never wanting to go back. I couldn't dance for those people anymore. The background dancers were leading my life, and that was not how it was supposed to be. That summer I learned I wasn't the wrong person; I had just made the wrong friends.

That wasn't the first time in my life I'd faced that problem. By the time I had reached my senior year of high school, all of my Christian friends had graduated and gone away to college. So I spent my last year of high school dancing with the world. At that time, I had an important choice to make: I could spend a year trying to dance like them, or I could spend a year trying to make them dance like me.

Thankfully, I chose the latter, even though it was the hardest. Being a Christian with non-Christian friends is not easy. Inviting your friends to church when you're in high school or college isn't as simple as it was during childhood. The older you get, the less likely it is they will want to come.

So the key to being a good witness is in how you live your life. When you are in a room full of non-Christians, every step of your dance counts. You have to take extra precautions to make sure your life is set apart and that you cannot be mistaken for a dancer of this world. The key to success in this area is not found in blending in with others, but in standing out. My friend Serena once told me, "Christians can do the most for the world when they become the least like the world." Nothing is divine about the dance of someone who goes to church on Sunday but lives like God does not exist during the other six days of the week.

Many young Christians walk away from God during high school or college. The Barna Research Group estimates that 50 percent of teenagers who currently attend church will not do so when they leave home. They choose to dance like the world, but in the end it catches up with them.

> *I think those of us who are raised in the church reach a certain point when we are trying so hard to find our independence and individuality that we try to break free from anything associated with our childhood— including our faith.*

Barna goes on to say that only 48 percent of born-again teens say they are absolutely devoted to the Christian faith.

I thought of this recently when I went out to dinner with some old high school friends. Fortunately, the three of us have remained pretty solid in our spiritual walks, but we remembered our friends who hadn't. We couldn't even count how many girls we knew who had gotten pregnant outside of marriage. Friends who had given into drugs and alcohol were now young victims of addiction. The saddest part of it all is that these were not friends from our public high school; they were our Christian friends who had served in leadership with us in our youth group. Some of them were led into sin by curiosity, others were led astray by giving into rebellion, and still others got off track by blurring the line between boundaries and compromise.

They were all people who were so on fire for God at one time that they thought they could never fall. But, actually, none of us is above falling, and we all need to safeguard ourselves against our weaknesses. Discover the things that tempt you—and flee from them. You cannot fall into sin if you remove yourself from the temptation.

When I was in high school, a youth pastor told me that at least half of the Christians I knew would turn away from God after they graduated from high school.

Yeah, right, I used to think. *My friends are pretty solid.*

But, according to both my experience and statistics from Barna, he was right. You are the only one who can keep yourself from joining those kind of statistics.

~ ~ ~

Proverbs 4:23 says, "Watch over your heart with all diligence, for from it flow the springs of life." During my last year of high school, I learned just how easy it was to slip into sin, so I guarded my heart firmly when I was around my unsaved friends. I was alert to what I was allowing into my heart and life. I made a few decisions that would keep me out of compromising situations.

For instance, I refused to go to any high school parties where drinking, drugs, and sex were going on. So on Friday nights I would drive to the football games alone and meet my friends there. All through the game I would listen to them talk about the upcoming party, and when the game was over I would go home while they went off to have the "time of their lives."

They all knew what I stood for and supposedly respected it, but every Friday we would go through the same ordeal. "Are you coming tonight, Shannon?"

"No."

"Well, you-know-who will be there, and he's asking if you're going to be there."

"No, guys, I'm not going."

"Suit yourself; you'll miss a good time."

On Monday morning the stories were always the same. So-and-so "hooked up" with so-and-so, and another so-and-so got so drunk he made a fool of himself. I never really regretted not going. I knew I couldn't graduate from high school halfway pure, so I took every chance I got to guard both my purity and my heart when I was around these people.

I knew going to the parties wouldn't make me drink or have sex or do anything else that I didn't want to do. But even if I didn't participate in those activities, it would send the message that I approved of the things these people did. That would have made me just like them. I would have been dancing their dance, and nothing divine would have been left in my steps when I was through. I had to wear my Sunday morning costume seven days a week in order to make a difference.

Another decision I made, and held fast to no matter how

hard it got, was not to date non-Christians guys or even Christian guys who were not as passionate about God as I was. Girls I knew were giving their virginity to Christians and non-Christians alike because they began to judge themselves by the world's standards.

I remember one conversation with a classmate that left me speechless.

"What happened?" I asked, amazed that she had given up her virginity as if it was no big deal.

"Oh," she replied, "we were home alone and it happened just like you see in movies. One minute we were casually kissing and the next we were having sex."

Horrified, I sat there pondering her words. At that point I realized just how differently Christians need to live. Most of my friends got into trouble by letting the world set their boundaries, instead of God's Word.

We don't realize how much the movies and television shows we watch affect us. Recently, my friends and I were watching a spy movie. "Kill him, kill him," my friend Katie and I yelled in unison at the TV. Later, as we talked, we realized that we were calloused to the concept of murder because we watch it on TV so often. The same applies for sex and self-image. Our standards can subconsciously be lowered and our idea of normal can be altered—all because we fail to guard ourselves.

I once heard a Christian speaker address the topic of compromise. He explained that Christians tend to "make deals" regarding sin. He pointed out that we justify sin by comparing ourselves to others. We make excuses like, "Sure, I make out with my boyfriend, but we're not *really* having sex." Perhaps we push the envelope when it comes to profanity, using words that closely resemble curse words. What we miss seeing is those who watch us from a distance cannot tell whom we are dancing for. We edge up next to that fine line between the secular and the sacred, and our convictions are blurred.

> *It starts with a single step, a mere flirtation with the world's ways, really, and before you know it, the show is over and the dancer is a mess.*

The world does not think as we think. People of the world may tell us they respect us, or even admire us. But trust me; the world will take any chance it gets to teach you a few steps of its own dance. Those who supposedly admire your choices will be the first to try to make you change your mind. That is how most strong Christians fall.

The main thing that can keep you from dancing away from God is a self-inflicted knee injury—get tough knees by being on them often in prayer. Our dance is not just simple enter-tainment—it's part of a war for our souls and for the souls of those around us. So we need to be on our knees in prayer.

I remember one conversation I had in high school with my friend Ruby. "I can't handle this," I had told her about a certain difficult situation I was facing. "I cannot take a step in any direction; I am just too tired."

"Maybe God wants you on your knees," she answered.

"I've been on my knees for weeks," I replied, exasperated.

"Maybe He doesn't want you to get up," she answered. Ouch.

Do you ever feel like that? Do you ever have days when you cannot dance because you cannot even stand up? When you are at your weakest, God is at His strongest, and that is when you will see Him lead you in the dance.

> *You need to pour your heart out so that you can work your life out.*

Surround yourself with friends who will urge you to do what is right. Don't take counsel from the ungodly.

During one of my early years of high school, a favorite guest youth pastor spoke to our youth group. We were surprised that his message was based on only one verse. Psalm 1:1 says, "How blessed is the man who does not walk in the counsel of the wicked, nor stand in the path of sinners, nor sit in the seat of scoffers!"

Now I know why that verse is so important. Five verses later, we're told, "For the LORD knows the way of the righteous, but the way of the wicked will perish."

My good friend Todd used to say, "It's one thing to have your boat in the water, and it's a completely different thing to have water in your boat." That's very true.

> *When your life becomes a war between purity and popularity, you have to be prepared to choose.*

The easiest way to be a good witness to your unsaved friends is to be prepared. We get ourselves in trouble when they catch us off guard. So know your standards. Know where to draw the line and when to say no—and be ready to draw the line or say no at any time. Tune your heart to the rhythm of God's heart every morning when you first wake up. Get in the Word; hit your knees before you even hit the dance floor. Listen to God, and talk to Him, too. Let Him coach you on the steps you will need that day. And then when the curtain falls and the day is done, let God know how it went—He'd love to hear from you.

> *It is one thing to be a Christian living out your convictions in this world; it is a completely different thing to be a Christian letting the world live out its convictions in you.*

When I was sixteen, I wrote the following words in my journal: "I will go forward alone with my God leaving *all* else behind. I will not lose sight of my goal or of my Savior. Because if I lose sight of my Savior, I will, in turn, lose myself."

Give up the glitter, girls, and hold out for the gold. When the world starts calling you for auditions, tell them they have the wrong number and hang up. Or as I used to tell the junior highers I worked with, "Say no, and then go." Don't stay around to flirt with the idea of sin.

The strongest dancer is the one who knows her weaknesses and works extra hard to protect those areas. If you know you have a weak ankle, you will probably wrap it before you practice.

If you know you easily fall into train-wreck relationships, then avoid flirting with unsaved guys. If you know you are an easy target for peer pressure, avoid compromising situations.

Many times the crowd you dance with determines how you dance. But occasionally people seem to stand alone, no matter who is beside them. Two examples come to mind, one good and the other not so good. Job was a man "blameless, upright, fearing God and turning away from evil," according to the first verse in chapter 1 in the book of the Bible named after him. He had it all—and lost it. The house was gone, the kids were killed, the animals were wiped out, and the bank accounts were drained. And to top it all off, Job's health became so bad that he could hardly stand to live.

> *During the times you tell yourself you cannot fall, you are most prone to doing just that. Knowing your weaknesses does not make you weak—it makes you wise.*

His friends joined him and blamed him for his own troubles. His wife told him to curse God and die (literally—check out Job

2:9). But Job refused to look at the feet of the ungodly; he refused to learn their ways and dance their dance. Instead Job did not sin or blame God (Job 1:22). "The LORD restored the fortunes of Job when he prayed for his friends, and the LORD increased all that Job had twofold" (Job 42:10). God will bless those who follow Him. He will reward those who stand strong and dance righteously, refusing to bend to the ways of this world.

> *But God will not bless the great pretenders*
>
> *of this world who think their costumes are*
>
> *enough to get them into heaven.*

God watches the feet of those who take the stage before Him; it's obvious who really knows the steps and who is just trying to play along. Look at Judas. He was one of the twelve apostles. He hung out with Peter, the "rock," and James and John, the "sons of thunder." He literally walked the streets with Jesus, and for thirty pieces of silver he sold his soul. It didn't matter who Judas's friends were; he apparently never heard a word any of them ever said, including Jesus.

He walked with God, he talked with God, and he danced with God—face-to-face. Yet he never looked down at Jesus' feet. He never learned the steps of those who belong to the Lord. So he tripped and fell and eventually killed himself. What a contrast. Many of the other apostles died as martyrs for the cause of Christ, yet Judas died lonely and guilty and unable to live with himself. He had all the right background dancers, but he never knew the dance.

Just like my friends who learned the steps of the secular dance, Judas made up his own song and danced to his own rhythm and eventually created his own misery. His very dance betrayed the Son of God. With their very feet, many people I grew up with danced right into heartache and sin.

And I, just like everyone else, have danced through my own stages of compromise. At moments I also got caught up in the glitter of the stage and almost gave up on the gold waiting in the Divine Dance. At moments I was so blinded by the stage lights that I couldn't see God, nor did I look for Him. But in those times, I learned my weaknesses, and I learned there is no shame in wearing wrist guards or ankle wraps. I learned when it was time to be strong and dance, because I was a witness to my background dancers as well as to my audience. I also learned when it was time to let the curtain fall and move onto another stage because the pressures of the world were too great.

Learn the rhythm of walking with God so well that you know it by heart. Know the answers to the hard questions before you are ever asked. Know your problem areas and safeguard yourself.

Be authentic, be different, and be bold. Dance the song of Job, no matter who tells you to curse God and die. Be a blessing to the unsaved people God has placed in your life. Give them a reason to want to dance like you. Don't preach to them, don't shun them, and don't pretend you approve of their lifestyles. Show them the secret of the Divine Dance in the way you live.

There is no shame in setting boundaries in

your friendships with the unsaved.

Actually, it is a very healthy thing to do.

You cannot control this world,

but if you are not careful, people of the

world can easily control you.

The secret to succeeding in the limbo between heaven and this world isn't in never missing a step. Instead, it's in letting God steal the show. So the next time the background dancers try to take over your performance, stand back and let the King of Kings and Lord of Lords take His rightful place as Lord of the Divine Dance.

Chapter 4

The Beauty of the Body:
Dancing in Harmony with Other Christians

I just want to be a wallflower, and I feel like I've been thrust out in the middle of the dance floor," a friend with an eating disorder told me. During a summer abroad in a third-world country, "Michelle" lost weight by a natural change in eating patterns. But the positive response to her new figure drove her to keep her weight down whatever the cost.

One night Michelle came to me in tears. She was tired of performing, and she wanted help. But even at a small Christian university she had to be careful whom she told about her eating problem, because of her fear of being judged. Michelle needed help, but she felt as if she had nowhere to turn. She felt even more pressure to stay thin from those around her—her fellow dancers were the ones seemingly driving her to ruin.

"She looks so good; I wish I could lose that much weight," our friend "Karen" said of Michelle.

I inwardly cringed. Knowing the truth but not wanting to make it public, I firmly told Karen, "I think she could actually afford to gain about ten or so pounds. She didn't need to lose that much weight and neither do you. She looked really good before."

After a slight hesitation Karen responded, "Yeah, I guess you're right."

But the chilling reality of the situation never really left me. How much of our performances are targeted at other Christians? How many times do we cause each other to fall instead of extending a hand to help? And how often do we compete against the very people who are on the same team?

> *When it comes to dealing with other Christians, oftentimes we find ourselves not loving each other—but shoving each other right off of the stage.*

In a place where harmony should rule and everyone should be at peace with each other, cutthroat Christians vie for the world's attention. And in one split second, God's chosen have forgotten their purpose and abandoned their calling. Almost subconsciously they slip into a familiar rhythm and resume the dance of this world. Competition reigns supreme, and the spotlight is quickly moved off of King Jesus and focused on the brawl going on among God's children.

> *You cannot forgive unless you forget,*
>
> *because former hurts will always sting*
>
> *until you close the wound.*

So how do we get beyond the pettiness of people and ignore the elbows that fly into our faces as we try to dance for God alone? First of all, we need to remember one simple rule of thumb: Our Christianity does not diminish our humanity. Christians are people, too. If God can love our Christian sisters and brothers as they are, then we need to learn to do it, as well. Instead of shoving one another, we must learn to dance with the rhythm of grace and follow the footsteps of Jesus as we forgive and choose to try to forget.

Sometimes the ailment is as simple as a stubbed toe, but at other times it is as critical as a broken heart. But the evidence of healing is always the same: You can tell you have truly forgiven someone when you no longer want to talk about how he or she has hurt you.

When I was in high school, a pastor told me that if I treated everyone I met as if he or she was hurting, I would be treating 90 percent of them correctly.

Proverbs 17:17 says, "A friend loves at all times." That means we are to love our friends even when they are not acting as if they love us. If someone steps on your toes, that is no reason to fling him or her into the orchestra pit. It's best when dealing with competitive Christians to remember that you're dancing for God, and all of the attention and glory should be His anyway.

> *Flying elbows are a cry for attention.*
>
> *They are a broken heart's way of saying,*
>
> *"Look at me; I'm special, too."*

Some people are just difficult, and their outbursts do affect your movements, but they should not *control* your movements. Someone else's bad attitude is not an excuse for you to develop a bad attitude, too. Even when you are being tripped and tried, you still have a choice. You can choose to glorify God with your reaction and bestow grace upon the one who is out of step, or you can choose to create an even bigger mess and dance out of step yourself.

One of the best biblical accounts of bickering and malice among God's people is in the story of two kings. Saul and David were each chosen by God to rule His people. David is the king who danced before God in the streets in his under-garment (remember him?), and Saul is the king who reigned before David. Saul held his crown so tightly that he chased and threatened David and ultimately took his own life in desperation. David danced for God, and Saul danced for his crown. Yet in their struggles David never turned on Saul to compete for the crown he was confident that God would one day deliver into his hands.

≈ ≈ ≈

So as dancers in the Divine Dance, we all need to learn to nurture the eternal and forget about the rest of it. No guy, no job, no moment of fame and popularity is worth the price of a destroyed relationship with a sister (or a brother) in the Lord.

But sometimes things go terribly wrong, and relationships are destroyed. Both sides leave wounded, and healing takes a long time. Although not giving in to the petty is the best way to avoid dissension on God's stage, sometimes the music of reconciliation is more applicable. Most of us have probably already suffered the severing of a godly friendship, and we know that the pain that started with a twisted ankle can grow into a serious injury with the potential to make you limp for a lifetime.

> *Christian sisters tend to fight often and over silly things. They fail to realize that the things they are fighting over are not eternal—but their friendship is.*

When this type of rift occurs, we need to learn some new steps before we can move on to the next number. We need to research, repent, restore, and release.

- First, we need to *research* the situation to see where things went wrong. It takes two to tango as they say, and all conflicts have at least two sides. We need to objectively evaluate the situation and perhaps get the insight of a godly mentor. When you turn to peers instead of mentors for advice in times like these, the situation usually turns into a gossip fest instead of a time for edifying eye-opening.

- Secondly, we must *repent*. Ask God for forgiveness, and then approach your friend. Ask for her forgiveness, too, even if she doesn't apologize. Apologize without seeking an apology from the other side.

- That flows right along with the third step of *restoration*. Romans 12:18 says, "If possible, so far as it depends on you, be at peace with all men." Try to make the friendship work. Allow room for healing and for new growth.

- And finally, once you have repented and taken the steps toward healing the hurt, you need to *release* it. You need to choose not to dwell on the memory of the incident that tore you and your friend apart. If your friend never forgives you, then so be it. You have done your part pursuing peace with all people.

Some people like to live in chaos, and they refuse to let things go. But these people tend to slow down—or even drop out of—the dance entirely, because the weight of their burdens becomes too much to bear. Psalm 37:23 says, "The steps of a man are established by the LORD, and He delights in his way." Make sure that all of your steps are ordered by the Lord and that He is delighting in your way.

≈ ≈ ≈

Some of you may think this is not very practical advice, but let me assure you that there is no quick fix to a rift among relatives—and that is what we all are in God's kingdom: relatives. People will disappoint you throughout your life. That will never change. But how you react can change as you grow in God's grace.

When I first left for college, I had never shared a room with anyone. I was used to having my own space and doing things my own way, so I started college with my little routine, all ready to start a new life. Little did I know how new some of it would be! Not only did I have a roommate, I also had thirty floor mates—and I had to share a bathroom and a washing machine with fifteen of them. Conflict? Oh, yeah, there was conflict, especially when someone emptied your freshly clean clothes out of the washing machine and threw them on the floor while they were still wet so she could use the machine next.

If God ever tried to teach me patience, it was during my two years of dorm life. But looking back, I realize I had more good times than bad. All thirty of us, for the most part, learned to get over the problems and irritations. As a result of being stretched you become flexible—or you break. In most cases God has to break you before He can stretch you, and often the finest tools He uses are our brothers and sisters in Christ. Everybody has rifts and everybody has problems. You will never be able to understand some things about some people, but you've got to learn to tolerate them.

I've had bosses, teammates, classmates, neighbors, roommates, and friends who have all ground at my nerves until nothing was left. They stepped on my toes and broke my heart, and sometimes they even blocked out the music in my life entirely. But in all of that I learned one of life's greatest lessons.

> *Each song has high notes and low notes,*
>
> *and no matter what, the dance goes on.*

Most of the time, friendships can be repaired after a fight. But sometimes they cannot. Sometimes rifts are God's way of telling us that it is time to let go of a relationship, or at least to change that closeness. Acts 15:36–40 tells us about Paul and Barnabas having a "sharp disagreement" over whether or not they should take John Mark with them on a missionary journey. Barnabas said yes, and Paul said no. As a result, two men who had been through so much together parted ways. Barnabas and John Mark went one way, and Paul and Silas went the other. But as a result, and because of their different destinations, they reached twice as many people with the gospel.

Sometimes it isn't even a fight that drives us apart from friends. Sometimes during curtain calls and costume changes, we realize we have to say good-bye. Life is full of transitions. Things change, and things change people. The people I am closest to in college are not my friends from high school; they are new people I met when I entered a new stage in life. These are the people I dance with, and they are the people who push me to be my best. And sometimes they just push me, but I love them anyway. It took me years to be ready to develop these kinds of friendships; I had to learn more than a few times what really matters and what doesn't.

❦ ❦ ❦

A lot of times we get frustrated with the other dancers on the stage because they try to hog the spotlight. But that wouldn't really bother us if we weren't trying to hog that spotlight, too! When we see others' weaknesses, we need to look for those same weaknesses in ourselves.

Jealousy is the most common fuel in the fire that destroys friendship, and it stems from a lack of contentment in our own lives. One of my roommates is getting married in a few months, and the other night we were both home at the same time (which rarely happens) and we were exhausted from our day. We plopped down on our couch with a stack of her bridal magazines and watched three wedding-oriented movies and laughed and had a great time.

I could have let my desire to have someone special in my own life prevent me from having some great "girl time" with my roommate. I could have gotten sad and pouted as we looked at bridal gowns, and she told me all about the one she ordered. I could have refused to listen as she talked about the plans for their extravagant European honeymoon, but I took pleasure for her in that moment. It was her turn to be happy, it was her moment to shine, and it was her time to dance—and I danced with her, and we had a great time. It was probably the most fun we've ever had together.

> *Sometimes God gives us friends who are mirrors that show us our own flaws so we can work at changing our flaws. And until we change, He will just keep bringing more mirrors into our lives.*

One secret to *having* great friends is to *be* a great friend. Look for people whom you want to be like and make friends with them. On Thursday nights I have a potluck Bible study at my apartment with fourteen girls who are completely different from each other except for one thing: They are all striving to be women after God's heart. When we get together, God's presence meets us because our hearts are set on Him. We get really excited about the great things happening in each other's lives, and we all get tears in our eyes when someone shares her heartaches.

Each week as we gather in my living room, I am amazed at the depth of their friendship. Sure, we all annoy each other and we get irritated sometimes, but they have really shown me that it took years for me to learn how to be a friend.

> *Part of being a friend comes from refusing*
>
> *to give up on other people.*

You need to dance with them, clap for them, and remind them why they are dancing—long after they have forgotten. You need friends who remind you of Jesus and friends who push you toward Him when you want to run away. When your friends do these things, be grateful. And when they don't, give them grace.

Look for the best in everyone; cultivate gifts in the people you love—and even in the ones you don't.

Sometimes their cheering keeps us going when we would otherwise give up.

But if you find that there is always more shoving than loving in some of your friendships, perhaps it is time to say goodbye. You don't need to have a fight or a formal split. Maybe you just need to silently bow out of this number and move on to another stage.

Christians share a stage for a reason—we are all part of telling God's story. We are all works in progress, but if each of us works to do our part, we will find that together we move to a rhythm that captivates any audience. Have you ever seen a beautifully choreographed dance performance? Nothing is as breathtaking as watching a group of people move together in perfect unison. First everyone sways to the left, then they step to the right, and then at the same time they all jump and twirl. It's a routine, it's practiced, and it is perfect. Solid Christian friendships take a fair share of practice and commitment, as well.

> *Be the friend you would want to have.*

Just remember that we are to forgive others as we have been forgiven (Ephesians 4:32). So buy yourself a box of Band-Aids, and learn to love those you dance with—I'm sure you've also stepped on a few toes in your day. The key to successful Christian friendship is humility, and the reason for broken relationships is pride. A lot of what you get out of your friendships depends on what you put into them, and at other times friendship depends on the amount of grace you dispense.

Sometimes I think dancers should wear shin guards like soccer players. At other times, I think they need the full-body padding that football players wear. But most of the time, we all need just a little more space and a whole lot of grace. Let your friends know you are not out to steal their spotlight, and keep your eyes fixed on the Audience you are truly dancing for.

> *We all need balcony people in our lives.*
>
> *You know the ones I am talking about—*
>
> *the people who sit in the balconies of our lives*
>
> *and cheer us on as we dance for God.*

If anyone knew what it was like to be shoved and stepped on, Jesus did. But His strength was in quietness and confidence—and according to Isaiah 30:15 yours should be, too. Sometimes the best friends we can have are those we find in unlikely places and make in unlikely circumstances. The twelve disciples were unlikely candidates to befriend a King, but Jesus chose them—flaws and all—for a purpose. The same

God who chose them also chose you and your friends to take the stage at this time in your life, so that in His strength (and not your own) you may all work together to glorify Him.

So what are you waiting for? Go get your friends and dance.

Chapter 5

Every Dancer Needs a Coach:
Dancing with Your Parents

Families can put a kink in the Divine Dance more quickly than anything or anyone else because they are completely out of our control. We do not get to choose our families like we get to choose our friends and our costumes. And at times I'm sure we all wonder what God was thinking when He placed us where He did.

Let's face it; most families are enough to drive anyone crazy. As I write this, I am visiting my family for Christmas. My cell phone and my E-mail account have been overloaded for days with messages from friends saying, "I can't handle being in such close quarters with my family any longer!" "My parents spend all day fighting with each other, and then they come pick a fight with my brothers and me." "My parents are putting rules on me, and I don't even live at home anymore."

And, "If my mom compares me to my sister one more time, I am going to scream." Funny how all of the Christmas cards with nice smiling family portraits show the opposite.

Every family is different. Even in my short lifetime, I have already accumulated an album full of memories. I have carried distinct things with me from every stage of the dance. Like snapshots that I carry in my mind, I remember going to work with my dad on Saturday mornings as a kid and stopping at the donut shop along the way. I remember the time my mom hit the roof because I wanted to start shaving my legs and wearing makeup. I remember getting in a slight wreck when I first learned to drive. And I remember moving to a new house on my first day of high school.

I have memories with my family that no one else has, and you have memories with your family that no one else has. We all have our share of good and bad. All families have hurtful things that they never talk about and embarrassing things that they will never be able to live down. If the halls of our houses—or the floorboards of our stages—could talk, I'm sure they would tell all kinds of stories.

It should be no secret to any of us that our stories are greatly shaped by our families. After all, it is our families that first tell us who we are. They're the first to clap for us, laugh at us, and pick us up again when we fall. Stage after stage, show after show, for the most part, our families never change—although sometimes we wish they would!

Anyone who has ever been to a dance recital, a play, or even a graduation ceremony knows the first thing you do when you get to your seat is flip through the program to find the name of the person you are there to see. And when you are performing you always save the program as a keepsake because there is something special about seeing your name in print—it automatically makes you a part of what is taking place. So what can we learn from the name that is on the program? How does our family background affect our performance in the Divine Dance? Inevitably, like it or not, our families are part of who we are.

> *We have a distinct role in our specific families that God gave exclusively to us because He knew no one else in the whole world could play our role any better.*

On my program you find the name Kubiak. When I think about my Kubiak side of the family I just have to laugh. One memory that stands out in my mind more than any other is the time that my whole family, probably twenty of us, met at the beach, all wearing white T-shirts and jeans so we could take a "nice family portrait." Picture it in your mind. It was a hot July afternoon in southern California, and the whole world was at the beach. People were staring, and I couldn't blame them. We were a spectacle. The day was absolute chaos. I was fifteen and mortified to be dressed like my entire extended family.

There were crying babies, wound-up children, and annoyed adults. My grandpa was trying to tell the photographer that he didn't want to stand in the water because he was returning his pants to the store later that afternoon and he couldn't get them wet. My aunt was chasing other people out of the water behind us saying, "This is just as much our beach as your beach, and we want to take a picture, so please move!" And my other aunt leaned over and whispered in my ear, "Our family really knows how to put the word *fun* in dysfunctional."

In all of my embarrassment I glanced up at the nearby lifeguard tower. There was a really great-looking guy, not much older than me, watching and laughing. I winced and he waved. I wanted to dig a hole in the sand and disappear. That day has now been officially cataloged as one of the funniest gatherings ever. I love my extended family—as long as they're around, I know I will always have something to laugh about.

When I think about the maternal side of my family, I have fond memories, too. I remember playing board games on every holiday, and I think of childhood days spent on a custom-built swing in my grandparents' garage.

Each family has its own story. You may come from a Christian family, a non-Christian family, a blended family, a broken family, a two-parent family, or an extended family all living on one stage—but no matter where you come from, your role is always the same: "Children, obey your parents in the Lord, for this is right" (Ephesians 6:1).

You are to model your love for the Lord in your love for your family; your obedience to your parents is a reflection of your obedience to Christ. Even if you're over eighteen and out of the house, you are still not off the hook. Your attitude toward your parents is a major reflection of your attitude toward Christ. If you have unsaved parents, then this is even more important because you are their window into a lifetime of salvation. What they see in you is what they will base their views of Christianity on. Perhaps you will be the person to lead the ones who gave you life into having eternal life.

⤳ ⤳ ⤳

Out of the numerous commandments God could have given, He chose to give us only ten. One of those commandments is to " 'Honor your father and your mother, that your days may be prolonged in the land which the LORD your God gives you' " (Exodus 20:12). So I guess that means disobeying our parents is right up there with murder, adultery, and idolatry. And as much as being at home may seem like being in prison at times,

I think we'd all be a little better off if we just obeyed this commandment. But the older we get, the more we wonder just where this line of obedience is and how we find our independence while obeying (or not obeying) this commandment.

I had a friend in college who was twenty-two and happily dating a nice Christian guy. But her parents didn't approve of her dating anyone while in school. Since she no longer lived at home, she felt the choice was really up to her. She continued dating the guy, and her parents stopped paying her college tuition. It was her choice and she paid for it—literally—and seemingly with no regrets.

⤸ ⤸ ⤸

Let's take a general look at the role that families play in our lives. Families go full circle with us. They are usually the only people who stand at both our kindergarten and high school graduations. They are the people who can remind us of all of the funny things we said when we were five, and one day they will all too eagerly remind us of the stupid things we did at fifteen. And because we begin our lives with our families, they have a key role in how we see ourselves today. In fact, situations within my own family first made me realize that I danced for other people.

The first person I ever started dancing for was my dad. He is a great man, and I love him a lot. We're very close. But my dad is not a great conversationalist. Instead of words, he speaks with his body language—and, man, can it be loud! But I communicate with words, so I went through the early years of my life performing for him and trying to be the best at whatever I did so I could win his approval. But time after time I found my greatest efforts were only greeted by what I considered to be his silence.

> *It took me years to realize that my dad was proud of me, and it took me even longer to realize that he wasn't proud of me because of what I did but because of who I am.*

I am his daughter. That's enough to make him proud.

I think each of us has someone like that in our families. There is one person you would do anything to please, but no matter what you do, your efforts seem to fail. I sent an E-mail to a friend a few days ago telling her that I was praying for her troubled relationship with her mom as she was home for the holidays. She wrote back saying that things were worse than ever. "She just wants me to be my sister," she said. "And as we all know I am not my sister, and this makes me a constant letdown to her."

A few E-mails later she told me she was dreading the family New Year's Eve trip, and I reminded her that sometimes the things we look forward to the least turn out to be the most fun.

"Thanks for the reminder," she wrote back. "I think I just need to change my attitude, and things will be fine." I was so proud of her when I read that sentence because she had learned one of life's greatest lessons (especially where family is concerned). I've heard that life is 10 percent what happens to you and 90 percent how you react to it. I can see how true that has been in my own life.

≈ ≈ ≈

I think a lot of times we underestimate the role that family plays in our lives. When God sent Jesus to earth, He didn't send Him as an adult who would wander around as a nomad. Instead, He put Him in a family and gave Him parents. God designed family because He thought it was important; in fact, family is so important to God that He has even structured all of Christianity as a family. God is our Father, and we are His children, so that means we will even have family in heaven. When God first created the Divine Dance, He knew that each of us would need coaches to guide us along the way.

Every good dancer needs a coach. Coaches guide you, teach you, share the wisdom and insight that they have learned over the years, and most importantly, coaches cheer the loudest whenever you take the stage.

And there is probably at least a little bit of both of your parents inside of you. Some traits, like big noses or bony ankles, are genetic; others are learned, like manners and discipline.

A coach has a role in forming your development and your performance. A parent has a pivotal role in who you are and in who you will become.

Almost every parent does at least one great thing in his or her career as a coach. For instance, Ruth, another good friend of mine, loves her adoptive parents. To her they are the only parents she will ever have. Instead of choosing to feel rejected like some people who have been given up for adoption would, she has chosen to feel accepted. And she sees that putting her up for adoption is one of the greatest things her birth mom could have done for her. Once again, how we view our families plays into how we interact with our families. Ruth has a great relationship with her parents, because she chose to develop a great relationship with them and to be grateful for them.

My friend Heidi, who grew up as a middle child, had a lot to say about family when I asked about her upbringing. "During my teenage years," she said, "my parents were simply authority figures to me. I thought it natural to make my own decisions, and I got upset if they put their foot down. I wasn't as responsible as I thought I was at the time. Looking back, I see that by treating all of us kids differently my parents helped me to find my place in the middle. Had they chosen to discipline me like they did my older brother, I would have laughed in their face and blown them off. Had they disciplined my younger sister the way they did me, she would have rejected them and closed herself off completely. My mom and dad knew what they were doing, even though it didn't look like it, because they were helping us develop as individuals."

> *Our relationships with our parents are two-sided. They coach and we dance, and if we really work together, we can make a great team.*

She went on to make an excellent point: "Now I view my parents as my friends for two reasons. First, because they helped me to feel accepted and trusted by them. And second, because of how much I worked at earning their trust and how much effort I put into being understood and how much I valued their efforts."

Usually when we think we can do without a coach, we find ourselves flat on our faces with nothing to show for our efforts. I really like to watch figure skating during the Olympics, and I will never forget the year that one of the greatest woman figure skaters fired her coach. She fired someone who had invested years in her career and who had, in a very real sense, made her who she was. Having been a previous silver medalist, this was the year this skater was to take the gold. But I cringed at the thought of her not having a coach, and in the end she lost the gold. Trying to do it on her own didn't cut it. She needed the extra insight; she needed the extra push. She needed that little bit of criticism that, if taken the right way, would have made her skate better. Sometimes, I think we all need those things, too.

At one point in my life, I put all of my energy into fighting with my mom instead of loving her or understanding her. I went out of my way to be difficult because I lived in her shadow and I wanted out. My mom is a women's retreat speaker and Bible study leader, and she is the one person anyone would really want to be like.

I was Becky's daughter, and that was all anyone could see when I walked onto the stage. As far as they were concerned, my mom and I wore matching leotards.

Here I was dancing for all of these people like a puppet on a string, and so one day I just cut the string. I exploded. When I finally calmed down enough to talk to my mom about what was actually going on, she was surprised. She had no idea about the pressure I faced as her daughter. The ridiculous expectations placed on my shoulders may have come from people she knew, but they definitely did not come from her.

> *But in my early adolescence, I was suffocated*
>
> *by the expectations put on me—*
>
> *not by my mother, but by those who knew*
>
> *the name that was on my program.*

Any of you who are pastors' kids, missionary kids, or kids with parents in any type of Christian leadership role probably understand what I am talking about.

A lot of times we place unnecessary burdens upon ourselves. We create certain roles for ourselves in an attempt to find our place within our families, and we kill ourselves trying to live up to our own expectations. But if you would sit down and talk to your parents about how you *think* they view you, and how they really *do* view you, you'd be surprised at what they would say. I think a lot of the issues that plague us throughout our lives come from the way we view our family life.

≈ ≈ ≈

As my friend Jessi pointed out, this brings us to a dangerous place. "When parents are not involved in their children's lives, or their roles are distorted, girls have to look to the world to fill the holes in their lives. That happened to me in my teen years. Because my father was distant, I looked to boys to fill the holes of male love, affirmation, and security that I was missing," she said. "I also looked to partying and my friends to fill the hole of a family because of the unstable and hostile environment that I had with my mom. Whatever people turn to in order to fill that void, they need to realize that it is not the love of the family that God intended it to be."

> *We expect our parents to be perfect,*
>
> *and we think they expect us to be perfect.*
>
> *And in our own eyes all of us walk*
>
> *around failing all the time.*

Jessi had to overcome a lot of pain within her family. Sometimes, in situations like Jessi's that seem hopeless, we need to remember that God placed us in our families to be a light and an example. Jessi is now married, and her Christ-centered wedding alone was a huge witness to her (mostly divorced) family about the value she places on marriage and family.

A lot of the bumps and bruises that come from dancing with our families are due to a lack of communication on both sides. Earlier I told you that my dad isn't a man of many words, and the older I get, the more I see that I don't exactly communicate well with him, either. Over the years, I have realized that sometimes I have a hard time communicating with him because I am so much like him. I don't think I realized just how true that was until I saw my dad in one of his weakest moments.

My dad grew up as the oldest of six kids, and as most big brothers and sisters quickly learn, it is easy to get lost in the midst of baby toys and midnight feedings. There's always another child to quiet or another mouth to feed. Because of this I think my dad grew up feeling somewhat unloved. This became especially apparent to me when we were all gathered at my grandpa's house looking through old pictures after my grandma's funeral. I had found a particularly cute one of my dad and asked my grandpa to put a date on it for me.

"We had fun with you when you were a baby, Kenny," he said to my dad with that faraway look of remembrance in his eye. "Your mother really loved you; she loved all of you kids."

Hours later, when my dad was alone with my mom and me, he brought the conversation to the surface once again. At fifty years old, it was almost as if my dad was trying to convince himself that he had been loved. Just as I had spent my life dancing for my dad's approval, he had spent his life dancing for his mother's love.

So knowing that my dad and I have communication problems causes me to work harder at being heard and being understood. Now that I am older, and I spend most of my time

> *Even when the outward applause isn't audible, it is still there. Sometimes the things we dance the hardest for are things that we have had all along.*

away from home, I regularly e-mail my parents to keep them updated on the events of my life.

Over the past several years, I have told them about things as trivial as getting an A on my Spanish quiz and things as important as wanting to change my major. Both of my parents are perpetual list makers, just like me. When I give them all of the scenarios of how the decisions I am making could possibly affect my life, that gives them confidence in my ability to make decisions. They know I am thinking things through and weighing the odds. They don't even flinch these days when I tell them I am flying to San Francisco for a weekend with friends or that I got accepted into an intensive journalism program in New York. Over time, by communicating with my parents, I have proven to them that I am capable of making my own decisions. Yet sometimes I still get frustrated when I send my dad a two-page E-mail only to get a one-word response. Like I said earlier, in families, some things never change.

My friend Katie offered me a little added insight in the area of communication. She said that one of the most important lessons she learned growing up was how to talk with her parents. When they would pelt her with a million questions about why she wanted to go to a movie instead of studying, and why she was going with certain people, she began to see that it was better just to give them an answer. That way she would actually get to go, whereas if she copped an attitude, she would wind up confined to the house.

Keeping your parents in tune with your dreams will also aid you in the Divine Dance. Often parents will do whatever they can to help you develop your skills and map out a game plan. Many parents want you to have every opportunity possible, and most parents want to give their children opportunities they never had themselves.

> *More often than not, your parents won't be surprised when you succeed, and they will be the first to stand up and clap for you when you make it to the big stage.*

Your parents aren't the enemies the world will tell you they are. They are people who will love you in a way that nobody else ever can. In the end, your parents cannot make your life miserable unless you let them. Most parents, though, don't try to make anyone's life miserable.

As your life changes, their roles change. That's a hard thing for both us and them to understand. They've been responsible for you for your whole life, and they will be held accountable to God for the way they raised you. Often they are not being nosy when they ask you questions; they just want to know who you are becoming as you mature.

> *You don't get mad when your friends ask what you are doing after school, so why should you tense up when your parents ask the same question?*

At this stage in the dance, your relationship with your parents depends more on how you view them and interact with them than on anything they really do. The steps of this dance may not always be the easiest to follow, but they always prove to be worth it in the end. When the music fills the air, and you glance down at your family name on the program of your life, remember that the key to growing up is found in loving, respecting, obeying, and communicating with your parents, as well as in having the right attitude.

I know dancing is not an Olympic sport, but if it ever is I'm sure the gold will go to the one who doesn't fire her coach. Don't give up on the name that is on your program, because when all of the awkward and difficult stages are behind you, families really do make the best of friends.

Chapter 6

Clothed in Righteousness:
Dancing with Integrity

Have you ever heard the saying "The clothing makes the man"? Well, in many ways, it's true. In stage performances, the costumes make the characters. I recently saw Disney's *The Lion King* on Broadway, and I was surprised by the costumes. They were so lifelike. As far as I was concerned, those were not people onstage performing; they were animals in the jungle. Because of the authenticity of the costumes, I thoroughly enjoyed the performance.

What do our "costumes" say about those of us in the Divine Dance? Do we bear the authenticity of Christ, or do we cheapen ourselves with the costumes of this world?

Just a quick glance at today's fashion magazines shows us that modesty is no longer in style. But if Christian girls would look at life as a dress rehearsal for heaven, fashion would quickly turn around. As high school and college women, you are young and impressionable, but you can also make a lasting impression on your generation and its trends.

What every dancer fails to realize is just how much the way she dresses says about her. Your clothing screams volumes about your character. This is one area in which Christians especially fall victim to dancing for this world. Nobody wants to be the nerdy girl who looks like she has gone shopping in her grandmother's closet, so we all end up with empty wallets and literally little to show for our efforts.

It seems to me that each time I go shopping, the clothing gets smaller and the prices get higher. How does that work? One of life's greatest mysteries, I guess. But what is not a mystery is God's standard for modesty, integrity, and honesty in the lives of Christians.

So let's toss *Glamour* and *Seventeen* out of the window for a second and see what the Bible has to say about how we should be clothing ourselves. Romans 13:14 says, "But put on the Lord Jesus Christ, and make no provision for the flesh in regard to its lusts."

Now I think most of us would admit that we don't keep Jesus on a hanger between our jeans and sweaters, but this verse is a lot more practical than that.

Our generation likes to walk the line. We throw dress codes out the window, and we try to bend the rules every chance we get. We want to be in style and look good so others will notice us. Even in Christian circles immodesty rules the day. Christian schools seem to have a hard time enforcing their dress codes, and young Christian girls dress in as little clothing as possible.

With questions like "How much cleavage is too much?" and rulers that measure to make sure that shorts and skirts just barely make the grade for school dress codes, Christian girls are selling themselves short and are buying into the trends of this world. We toss purity out the window in return for popularity. Many times we get up on the stage and take off the righteous garments Christ has clothed us in, and we are left standing naked before an audience that doesn't really care. I think we are so willing to be immodest in our outfits because we have forgotten who we are. We are daughters of the Most High God; we are princesses from the line of the King of Kings. Princesses do not dress like women off the street who are selling their bodies.

As a daughter of the King, you are expected to dress and act like a princess at all times— not just on Sunday mornings when you find yourself within the palace walls.

If you have great abs, good for you. If you have the perfect figure, thank God for it. If your jeans fit in an ideal way, praise God for that. But whatever you do, don't use it as an excuse to cheapen the royal blood that flows through you. A princess has enough self-confidence to know she is important and realizes she is a role model—so she dresses accordingly. A princess has too much class to wear clothes that would take men's minds off her rank and who she is—and put the focus on her body.

The biggest problem with Christians and clothing is that our thinking is off. We forget that our clothing defines the way others see us. We forget that we are dancing not for the applause of men, but for God's applause. We forget that the point of our lives is to lead others to Him, and if they do not see an outward difference in our lifestyles, then they will never see the inward difference in our hearts. Sometimes the message of Christ's death on the cross is lost because we have adorned ourselves in so much glitter that people cannot see Jesus.

I am not talking about trading in the latest fashions for a set of "Jesus freak" T-shirts, but I am talking about being cautious and conscientious in your style. It may not be easy, but you can look a little harder when you are at the mall to make sure you find shorts that cover your bottom completely. You can try on a sweater with a higher neckline or one that isn't skintight, and look just as good (and really even better). You cannot dance the Divine Dance in a costume that is anything less than divine.

Have you ever been on vacation in a foreign city or country and noticed just how much your clothing made you stand out? Sometimes you can almost hear the outfits of tourists screaming, "I'm not from around here!" And in a subtler (and less tacky) way, as Christians, we should have wardrobes that say the same thing.

Wait a second, Shannon, you may think. *Man looks at the outward appearance, but the Lord looks at the heart, so why does my wardrobe have anything to do with my Christianity?*

As Christians, we are called to a higher standard. The bar has been raised, and we dance to a different beat. So going back to the Romans 13:14 passage, let's take a closer look at what making "no provision for the flesh in regard to its lusts" means. Just as dancers in recitals choose their costumes to reflect the characters they are portraying, our clothing, too, reflects our character.

> *The way you dress, the way you act, and the way you talk have everything to do with your walk with the Lord because your outward appearance is a reflection of the inward state of your heart.*

In high school I was known as somewhat of a Goody Two-shoes, especially among the popular kids I hung out with. But one day, I decided to break out of my mold and wear a rather small halter top to school. I certainly got a lot of attention that day—but not the kind of attention I wanted. My friends were surprised, the guys made suggestive comments, and I was embarrassed. And I learned an important lesson—clothing can never make you beautiful, but it can make you cheap. What you advertise you are expected to produce.

If you want to wear a shirt that doesn't really cover anything, then don't be surprised when the guys you meet want to see even more than you are willing to show—and don't be surprised that they think you will show it to them. One of my friends' moms used to say, "Don't let the eye see what you don't want the hand to touch." Holiness needs to be our goal at all times. I'm not saying you have to cover every square inch of your body, but going that extra mile to cover that extra inch will do you a lot more good in the long run. If you're embarrassed to wear something around your parents or your grandparents, you probably shouldn't wear it at all. If you wouldn't wear that skirt or that top if you were going to hang out with Jesus, then you shouldn't wear it anywhere.

Instead of always pushing the limit and wondering how much we can get away with, we need to put that extra energy into making sure that we project a godly image. If we are defined by our clothing, then we need to make sure that our clothing is defining us as godly and holy women made in God's image.

If this is a big struggle for you, maybe you need to evaluate the motive behind your wardrobe. If you want to turn heads, you probably will. But will your clothing show others what a relationship with Jesus truly looks like? Or will it suggest a different type of relationship? If you are wearing something that will cause those around you to lust, then you haven't let the words of Romans 13:14 sink in. Guys think differently than we do.

Bare midriffs, cleavage, and bottoms falling out of shorts won't produce godly character in you or those around you. And it won't attract it, either. Your costume makes all the difference in your performance.

> *If people are so distracted by what you are wearing (or what you aren't wearing), then they will never see you, and they most certainly will never see God in you.*

As Christians, we have a responsibility to the rest of the world. We can show that although life may be a dance, it doesn't have to be a strip routine. On a recent trip to the bookstore, I glanced through some magazines and found a quote that saddened me. An eighteen-year-old girl was quoted as saying of Jennifer Lopez, "Hey, anyone who can own a restaurant, design clothing, star in movies, record music, get divorced twice, and finally get engaged to her true love—and still look beautiful after all the hard work—is definitely an inspiration to me."

If J. Lo's tendency to leave little of her body to the imagination is our beauty ideal, it's not surprising our perspective is off-kilter. God's vision of true beauty is vastly different. One way we can model that difference is in our dress.

～ ～ ～

I remember taking a missions trip to Europe when I was in high school. Pornography was everywhere in the country we visited, and it was starting to trip up some of the guys on our team. So one night before we went to bed, the guys covered up the posters and flyers on the walls of our hostel. Finally, the images were out of sight and out of mind. Guys who are striving to be godly will look for girls who are striving to be godly.

A lot of times, clothing is what attracts (or doesn't attract) us to other people. Haven't you ever seen a good-looking guy wearing really dorky clothes? Most of the time it makes you wince and turn the other way. Or how about your parents? Don't they own at least one article of clothing that embarrasses you every time it comes out of the closet? What if the reputation of you and your family was based on that one horrid piece of clothing? I don't think it would be accurate, and worse, I think you would be mortified. If a family dresses like they are poor, people will think they are poor. If a family dresses like they are rich, people will think they are rich. And if a family (or family member) dresses like they are cheap, then people will think they are cheap.

> *Sure, guys may look at you if you are baring all, but they certainly will not take you home to meet their mothers.*

What if someone's opinion of God's kingdom was based entirely on you and how you dressed and behaved? Would your life accurately reflect someone striving toward the glory of God? You know, some people point out that "your life is the only Bible some people will ever read."

I can't be held responsible for what other people think of the way I dress, you may think. But an important part of being a Christian is about being above reproach. The costumes used in the Divine Dance are integrity and purity. It will not always be easy to strive toward righteousness. It won't always be easy to dress for God's glory. But God designed you, and He knows your true beauty. He wants His glory and beauty to shine in us and through us—but a lot of time our own vain strivings prevent that from happening. Remember, you were made in the image of God. Does your clothing acknowledge that you are aware of that fact?

Looking at society, it is no wonder we all fall into these traps. Every year actresses bare their bodies for the world to see, and magazines create polls on the public opinion of these women's clothing. Musicians get up on stages in really small outfits at concerts, take even more off as their performance goes on, and the crowd goes wild. But this does not give us an excuse. We know better and we should live better. After all, the only audience we should be concerned about is God.

The only things from this life that will carry over into the next are the things that we do for the Lord. The only thing we get to take to heaven with us is other people. We don't get to take a suitcase full of trendy clothes. In a very real sense, Christians need to view this life as a dress rehearsal for heaven. So put on the Lord Jesus Christ. Sparkle with His purity.

Ephesians 4:24 says, "And put on the new self, which in the likeness of God has been created in righteousness and holiness of the truth." Take off the costumes of this world. Raise the bar. Bring purity back into style. Bring integrity to the front of the stage. Remember your Audience of one, and forget about the rest. He knows you better than the rest; His garments aren't passing trends. He has tailor-made a costume just for you. Will you wear it? Will you listen to the Coach of all coaches when He tells you that your costume will make or break your performance?

Next time you find yourself flipping through the latest catalog or surfing through the racks of your favorite store, remember fashion isn't a crime—but bad fashion is. Invest as much time into putting on the fruits of the Spirit as you do putting on your clothes and your makeup.

> *Love, joy, peace, patience, kindness, goodness, gentleness, faithfulness, and self-control will all still be in your garment bag in heaven— what you buy in stores won't be.*

You may stand almost naked before man today, but you will stand naked before God in heaven. Let Him clothe you in the righteousness He desires to give you. Let Him cover you with His love and continue to fashion you in His image.

Let the Author of the dance be the Author of your life, and let your costume be evidence that you are a daughter of the Most High God and that He is residing in you as you abide in Him.

Dance with passion. Dance with poise. And dance with purity.

Chapter 7

Wanting to Tango:
Dancing with Dating

*A*s the music softly floats around you, and your fellow dancers begin to pair up and dance together, leaving you all alone, you can begin to feel abandoned. You want to be invited to dance so badly that you will say yes to anyone who asks you. Nothing is worse than being the only one not dating, right? Wrong. I learned the hard way that one thing worse than not dating is dating the wrong guy.

Never let the fear of being alone cause you to cling to the first guy who walks by. I did that, and as a friend of mine once said, "We don't count that as a dating relationship. We count that as a mistake." Dating the wrong guy will always be a big mistake.

In my first semester of college, I got caught up in the "ring by spring" mentality. Every professor I had joked about the possibility of meeting a mate in his or her class. Many chapel speakers tried to give how-to advice on finding a spouse. I wasn't really ready to get married, and I certainly wasn't looking to find a husband at eighteen years old, but at a school with a three-to-one girl-to-guy ratio, I didn't want to get left behind. So I dated the first guy who came along. But after a short dating stint with the wrong guy, I have spent the past several years single by choice. I'm no longer willing to settle for just anyone.

≈ ≈ ≈

Being a Christian should always be the first prerequisite for any guy you date, but it should not be the only one. Christian guys can be all wrong for you, too. Just because he is a Christian does not mean he is the one God has for you. Look for common interests; look for someone who is going in the same direction in life. Don't look for someone you can live with; look for someone you cannot live without. Look for a man of passion and integrity, with a love for God so strong it is evident in everything he does and says—even dating.

> *Look for someone who holds you in such*
> *high regard that your purity is a*
> *priority in his life.*

God pairs each of His dynamic duos up in ways that are as unique as each of the couples.

As I write this, many of my friends from high school and college are married or engaged—it is like a disease swept through the land, and I'm the only one who didn't catch it. Perhaps you are just beginning to date, or maybe you have been dating for years. Or maybe you are still waiting for the opportunity to date—but no matter where you are, one thing is for certain: Everyone wants to tango, and nobody wants to be the last one asked to dance.

So when it comes to dating most of us have to ask, "What is God up to?" Although I don't have all of the answers, I've learned there is no formulaic pattern. But there are a few principles that trace back to the days of the Bible that you might find very helpful.

In all of God's great love stories, you find the same ingredients. The first ingredient you'll find is a man of God. A man of God is willing to seek God first and then pursue the woman he loves. Let's look at a father-and-son team who saw God's hand when it came to love.

Abraham sent his servant to find a bride for Isaac, but with so many women to choose from and a fear of being rejected, Abraham's servant offered a prayer. In Genesis 24:14, he says, " 'Now may it be that the girl to whom I say, "Please let down your jar so that I may drink," and who answers, "Drink, and I will water your camels also"—may she be the one whom You have appointed for Your servant Isaac; and by this I will know that You have shown lovingkindness to my master.' " Notice that Abraham's servant prayed as he set out to seek a woman for Isaac. Rebekah's only role was to be hospitable. God put her in the right place at the right time and made her an answer to someone else's prayer.

The second ingredient is a godly woman.

A godly woman trusts God and waits for His guidance in her life.

Today's society is missing the mark. With a recent surge of reality dating shows, people knock themselves out to go on national TV to find a soul mate. Women are willing to join a pool of twenty or twenty-five women who are all vying to seduce one man. No wonder these relationships don't last long after the show's finale.

Yet how many times do we fall into similar patterns?

Game playing kills honesty in relationships.

This is especially true during prom time. I remember prom season all too well. It can be a really fun time—my senior prom was a blast. But it can also be a time of intensified stress and manipulation. A girl I knew spent weeks zeroing in on one poor guy—doing everything in her power to get him to ask her to the prom. She bought him gifts, left him notes, and even called his house. She succeeded in being asked, but she didn't have a very good time. Nothing is right about a date or a relationship in which the woman is the pursuer.

≈ ≈ ≈

Back in our biblical analogy, years later when it was time for Isaac and Rebekah's son to pick a bride, Jacob also sought God. He saw Rachel and was instantly awestruck. So Jacob vowed to win her love. He bargained with Rachel's dad and agreed to work seven years in return for Rachel's hand in marriage. In Genesis 29:20 we find these words, "So Jacob served seven years for Rachel and they seemed to him but a few days because of his love for her." What romantic words! God sure does know how to write romance. Jacob's love for Rachel was so deep that when his father-in-law cheated him in that deal, he agreed to work another seven years in order to have Rachel as his own. Notice that this godly man was a man of his word, and he worked hard to win his bride.

The third element in all of God's great love stories is time. God usually likes to take a lot of time—and why not since He literally has all the time in the world? If God is going to knit two different hearts together "until death do us part," then you'd better believe it will take Him some time. Just like the rest of your body, your heart matures over time. Like two seeds, God waters the hearts of the two He desires to join together and watches love grow. But sometimes other fruits need to be cultivated in both hearts separately before love can grow in their hearts together. That's usually all God needs: a godly man (willing to prayerfully pursue), a godly woman (willing to sit back and wait to be pursued), and a little bit of time. All of the other ingredients are usually exclusive to each individual story.

⤚ ⤚ ⤚

Now wait a minute, you might be thinking. *I'm not looking for a lifetime commitment; I just want a date for Friday night.* But the same rules still apply. These days people seem to want a quick fix for everything. Girls would rather dance with anyone to avoid the risk of standing alone. Women have become the pursuers out of fear of being left out and unloved. Some girls are marrying extremely young for fear of never finding anyone else. That is not how God intended for love to be. Human love, in the union of marriage, is a metaphor for His love for us.

Notice that in all of God's great love stories, He sends the man to search for the woman with the purpose of marriage in mind. Anytime between fifteen and twenty years old, you cannot expect to be ready for marriage. You can't even expect a boy to be a man. Give the guys around you time to grow into godly men. And whatever you do, don't pursue them. Have you ever watched a couple dance when both of them were trying to lead? What a mess. They step all over each other's feet, and they both walk away sore and confused. Wait for a man that is willing to be bold enough to pursue you, and let him lead. Otherwise nothing will be as it should in your relationship.

Even if you are too young to get married, you are not too young to make wise choices. Have some fun, but don't get too serious too fast. I look back through all of my old journals sometimes when I come home to visit my parents. I can't help but laugh at the things I thought just a few years ago. It seems that settling down and getting married filled my mind. Now it seems that other things are on my mind. Yes, I'm still waiting for God to bring me a great love story, and I am praying for my future husband, but I'm not sitting by any phones. I'm enjoying life and serving God and taking advantage of the years I will otherwise lose.

We don't always know what God is doing in our lives, and we are always unsure about whom He will write into the next chapter of our story. It's okay to be unsure about the guys in your life. Grab a burger or hang out with some friends. But the second you see that the guy is less than what you want, break it to him gently and let him go. It will hurt less for both of you that way. Holding on to the wrong guy may prevent you from being able to embrace the right one. When I meet new guys, I often measure them against the list of what I am looking for in a relationship.

I'm reminded of the scene in the movie *You've Got Mail* when Meg Ryan's character and her boyfriend are breaking up. She asks him if there is someone new in his life and he says yes. When he asks her if there is someone new in her life, she pauses, then answers, "No, but there's always the idea of someone else."

If you know someone is not whom you are looking for, then you don't want to waste his time or yours. Hold out for the "idea" of someone who is right for you, the one God has for you.

When it comes to romantic love, that's an awkward dance to learn. It involves shyness, embarrassment, and lots of uncertainty. But trust that the same God who is writing the story will teach you each step as you need to know it. However, before you can learn to dance with another—especially such close steps—you must learn to dance alone. If you want to find a godly person, you must be a godly person.

All of the dating books I read in high school were written by someone who was already married. *Easy for you to say,* I'd think as I read their advice. *You've forgotten what it feels like to be the only one sitting at home on a Friday night.*

So I'm going to give you some practical advice from my perspective of currently being single. Although I have never been really serious about anyone, I have been on enough dates, and lived vicariously through enough friends, to learn a few tricks of the trade.

When it comes to dancing and romance, I think all of us will agree that we usually feel our most important audiences are usually the guys that come into our lives. We tend to dance for them in ways we wouldn't dream of dancing for our parents or our friends. We consider them worthy of our highest efforts.

Galatians 1:10 talks about this very thing: "For am I now seeking the favor of men, or of God? Or am I striving to please men? If I were still trying to please men, I would not be a bond-servant of Christ."

Dancing for the guys who enter the audiences in your life will only distract you from the Divine Dance. As I was growing up, I watched too many friends change their identities and plans for the guys they were dating. I had friends who gave up college to date a guy, gave up ministry to date a guy, and even gave up friends to date a guy. And I always wanted to ask later, "Was it worth it?" When my turn came, and a guy I dated briefly in college gave me an ultimatum to either give up my dreams and goals or give him up, I walked away from him quickly and confidently.

God did not make you half of a person; He made you a whole person just as you are. He has dreams and plans for you. When the best time comes, Mr. Right will fit into those dreams and plans, and he won't want to change them. So move in the direction that God has for you, and don't be afraid of going it alone. No matter how many of your friends get paired off and waltz around you completely in love, God is still with you and He is still at work.

The dance that usually bridges singleness and marriage is hard to learn. It is known as contentment. Contentment is being so absorbed in dancing for God and trusting Him so fully that you realize you have everything you need for this leg of the dance.

> *Contentment is not being full to the brim;*
>
> *contentment is acknowledging what you lack*
>
> *and being okay with dancing without it.*

The dating books I read seemed to say that contentment was found in not wanting a boyfriend, but I always felt I was lying to myself when I said that. Now I know true contentment in that area lies in simply being okay with not having a boyfriend. In practical terms, it means not wanting to hand every guy you meet an application to be your husband and to hold off on scheduling interviews.

Being human, we may wane in and out of seasons of contentment. Sometimes loneliness can eat away at the human heart like nothing else in this world. You can become so sick of being alone that you will take whatever attention you can find. So you get up on the stage with a mission in mind: to find love in whatever form you can. This is when life gets dangerous. Those who dance for attention always seem to get it, although it is not the kind of attention their hearts were really searching for. My mom used to say, "What you win him with is what you will keep him with." So if you enter a relationship based on something like outward appearances, that relationship will change when your looks change.

> *But if your heart is set on serving God,*
>
> *and somebody falls in love with God inside of*
>
> *you, he will continue to love you forever*
>
> *because God will reside in you forever.*

Timeless relationships are based on timeless principles. Nothing is as much fun as sitting down and laughing about old times with friends who have shared a good part of the Divine Dance with you. Imagine building a lifetime with someone when you don't have friendship in that picture. That would result in a marriage in which each half of the couple is living a separate adventure. There's no fun in an adventure that is not shared. That's why people always tell us it is best to be friends first. In Song of Solomon, one of the most romantic books in the Bible, the Shulammite bride introduces her lover: " 'This is my beloved and this is my friend' " (5:16). Don't you desire to say that someday, as well? I sure do.

All relationships build over time, but today we live in the microwave era. We want everything, and we want it now. But we fail to realize God's delayed responses are not always "no" answers. Sometimes they simply mean, "Not yet." So if you think that God has somehow failed you because He didn't say yes when you asked Him to give you that guy in your chemistry class, relax and be confident that God knows just what kind of chemistry you need for a love that will last a lifetime.

> *Your focus needs to be on being a godly woman, not on finding a godly man and then praying him into your life.*

The God who made you knows whom He has made for you. So your job is to do your homework. In talking of a godly woman, Proverbs 31:25 says, "Strength and dignity are her clothing, and she smiles at the future." She has the strength to say no to anyone less than God's best. She has the dignity to wait and be pursued instead of pursuing, and she smiles at the future, knowing that even if she is the last of her friends who learn to tango, God is up to something good on her behalf.

Proverbs 31:10 says, "An excellent wife, who can find? For her worth is far above jewels." Set yourself on the path of righteousness and refuse to dance the same dance as the world does in its dating dance. Serve God, use your gifts, and be that godly woman who will be a treasure to be found. After all, in Exodus 19:5 God says, "If ye will obey my voice indeed, and keep my covenant, then ye shall be a peculiar treasure unto me" (KJV). And there is a peculiar-shaped hole inside of your heart that God will one day fill with the treasure He has picked out for you. Don't lose hope.

⤸ ⤸ ⤸

Like I have said earlier, God's will is not always immediately discernable. You will probably meet and interact with several guys before you find "the one." Mr. Right doesn't usually come into your life accompanied by soft music and a cherub with a bow and arrow. So do yourself a favor as you wait for his arrival. Make a list. Not a complicated list, but a specific one. Write down five or ten absolutely nonnegotiable characteristics that your future husband must have. Then write down five things that are absolutely nonnegotiable that your future husband cannot have. Prayerfully consider the items you write down, and then pray those things for your husband whenever you think of him. Each time some guy waltzes into your life, pull out your list and see how he measures up.

Be honest with yourself, and you will save yourself a lot of heartache. Try to make your list one full of character traits. . . remember what he wins you with he will have to keep you with, and looks change over time. Add things like, "Must be able to make me laugh." And "Must not have violent bouts with anger." Make sure that any guy you date will hold you to an even higher level of purity than you would want to pursue for yourself.

If you are ever in a position of offering excuses for your actions, then chances are you feel a *need* to make excuses for those actions. A need for excuses usually stems from feeling that we have done something wrong. "Well, he spent the night, but nothing happened" is one I hear a lot. Even if nothing did happen, the fact that you are explaining your actions indicates trouble. A lot of things wind up happening unexpectedly because people weren't careful.

Compromising situations will eventually result in compromise, so avoid them at all costs. Hold out for the man with standards higher than your own—nobody can ever treat you too much like a princess, although many of us settle for ones who don't even treat us like princesses at all. Love is patient—

it doesn't rush into kissing, it doesn't fall into sex, and it doesn't threaten the reputation of a godly young woman.

Be careful how much you give away to the guys in your life. Each person you date, each guy you dance for, will take a piece of your heart (and maybe more) with him when he exits your stage. As godly women, we do not want to invite the one we marry to reside in the ransacked, trampled garden of our hearts. We want him to be able to rest in the shade of the big green trees that we have carefully nurtured just for him. When the one who matches your list and fills the hole in your heart comes, you will know. Maybe not right away, but God will tell you in His timing. But until then, keep the garden of your heart locked up tightly. Song of Solomon 4:12 says this about a godly woman's heart: " 'A garden locked is my sister, my bride, a rock garden locked, a spring sealed up.' "

The older you get, the more frustrated you may become. But in the end it will all be worth it. Sometimes the hardest part is holding on for the last few moments of the dance of singleness. You're exhausted, and you just want to quit. But if you can finish this song, God will let you tango somewhere in the next act.

Even in dating you must remember what this Divine Dance is really all about. It's a love story bigger than the tango. It's about God loving us so much that He called us apart and saved us. The Divine Dance is about our returning that love and reaching out to those who are still lost. Sometimes the tango becomes a part of that message, and two people can serve God together, but in the meantime don't do anything that will compromise your ability to tell God's story. Don't try to tango with the world. Don't "missionary date" (go out with non-Christian guys using the excuse that you're trying to win them to Christ). And don't just flirt with anyone. Your own spiritual health depends on it. Safeguard yourself against anything other than God's absolute best by refusing to take part in it. There is never an excuse for being unequally yoked or for being in a sexually immoral relationship.

If the guys in your life do not guard your heart like brothers, then they will never make good lovers or husbands or even boyfriends. Look for a man who models Christ. Look for one who holds you in high regard. Look for someone who is already dancing the Divine Dance, and dance with him. Set your standards high, and let God lift you to a level where you can attain them.

So whether you are tangoing today or waiting for tomorrow, keep this in mind: God desires what's best for you. He wants to give you a relationship that will model His love for you in earthly form. He did not spare His Son Jesus the first time around; I don't think He'll short you this time, either.

A good dancer knows that in any performance, no move is as powerful as the pause. So if you feel like you are in between woman and child, single and in love, then practice patience and become a godly woman as you learn the art of the divine pause.

Chapter 8

The World Is Your Stage: Dancing in the Darkness

God has a specific purpose in mind for each of us. Before He even set to work molding us in our mothers' wombs, He had great plans for us. Psalm 139:13–16 talks of God fashioning us and forming our inward parts. When I picture that scene, I see God lovingly putting each of us together and saying things like, "This is Shannon, and she shall be a writer; this is Rebecca, and she shall be a teacher. . . ."

God knows us. He knows our dreams, our goals, our strengths, and our weaknesses. He has given each of us talents with which to give Him glory. And He has given each of us a candle to light the way in a dark and dreary world.

Christians are to dance upon the world's stage. I hope you have gotten that point by now. But we are to dance upon the world's stage for God, and we are to bring His message of salvation with each step we take.

The greatest thing about college for me was meeting so many people with different gifts who will accomplish awesome things all over the world in their lifetimes. In some small way, I get to be a part of what God is doing in many different places through my friends' lives.

I think one of the most quoted (and greatest) movies of all time is *Chariots of Fire*. In one scene, Olympic runner Eric Liddell turns to his sister and says, "God made me fast, and when I run I feel His pleasure." Each of us has something different that was given to us by God so that we may feel His pleasure in a personal and amazing way.

When I write I feel God's pleasure. I get lost in my work, and I can honestly feel the Spirit of God moving within me as the words pour onto the page. My friend Amy, who is involved with the children's ministry at her church, feels the same way about working with kids. Her greatest joy is to see a room full of children worshiping God and memorizing the Bible. My roommate Jamela feels that way about art. She makes beautiful pieces that hang on our walls, and each one reflects God's glory. If you were to ask my friends and me why each of us does what we do, we would answer, "Because this is what I was born to do."

Sometimes we Christians make the mistake of thinking God only wraps His gifts in "holy packages," but that is not true. Not everyone is called to be a pastor or foreign missionary. We serve a God of limitless boundaries, and He has great plans for every gift He gives.

> *Everyone has significant gifts, all of equal importance, with which to worship God. But uncovering those gifts in our lives isn't always easy to do.*

Once my friend Heidi and I were talking about our futures. She grew up as a missionary kid in Germany and came to the U. S. for college, but her heart has never left the mission field. She hopes that after college she can start a coffee shop ministry somewhere in Europe so people can come in and get some coffee and hear the gospel.

Recently, God gave her a job in a coffee shop here in the States so she can gain the skills she will need on her journey. I'll never forget what she said as we sat talking one day sipping coffee. "I have learned a lot about God's gifts lately," she said. "I absolutely love making these menus and thinking of ways to decorate the shop. It's just so much fun to me, and I never really knew that God had gifted me in this way."

Heidi is a big hit in the coffee shop where she works

because she is friendly and cares about the people who come in. She reflects God in her coffee-cart service, and people notice. I'm sure many in Europe will come to Christ someday because of Heidi's warm coffee and her equally warm heart.

> *You are part of God's divine plan,*
>
> *and He has a purpose for you.*
>
> *The stage of your life has been set just*
>
> *to His liking. The costumes are perfect,*
>
> *the backdrop is just as He planned,*
>
> *and the audience that needs to be ministered*
>
> *to is in place. The only question left is:*
>
> *Is the dancer ready?*

Coffee mugs, laptop computers, and art brushes and easels are not necessarily holy things. But when placed in the right hands, they become tools for God's glory. Almost anything can become a tool for God's glory, but we often fail to realize that. We get up on the stage of life and see people with all of these other gifts, and we try to mimic them instead of letting God use us for the purpose He had in mind. When I first started college, I remember that everyone I met wanted to be a teacher, and I wanted to be a writer. There were many moments when I considered abandoning my calling to be just like everyone else. I'm really glad I didn't because I am definitely not a teacher.

But I know what it is like to be the only writer in a room full of teachers or the only ballerina in a room full of tap dancers. That isn't always easy. You may look around you and feel completely alone in whatever you want to do. You may be embarrassed to get up on the world's stage and dance because your dance is choreographed a little differently than everyone else's. But if you don't dance the way you were made to dance, God will be robbed of some of His glory. Better to dance to a different beat than to dance to one that just isn't you.

God didn't give you your gifts so you could sit on them and let them go to waste until you are old and gray. He gave them to you so you could use them now. Your youth is an asset to whatever gifts you possess, because it means you can spend your whole lifetime using your gifts for God's glory. I think many of us tend to view high school and college not as stages on which to dance but merely as bridges to cross. We view these short intervals not as places themselves but as roads to other places. But what if the bridge is all you get? What if, for you, there is no other side? What if God calls you home before you get to the place where you decide you're old enough and experienced enough to serve God? Then your bridge counted for nothing.

So what's your bridge counting for? What can you do today that you are putting off until next year? What gifts are lying dormant in your life because you are too lazy, too busy, or too scared to use them? What do you want to accomplish for God in your lifetime that you can start working on right now?

If you're a singer, then let us hear your voice. If you are a teacher, start in Sunday school where plenty of kids need you right now. If you are a writer, then let us read your words. If you are a dancer, then let us see your feet. But most importantly, if you are a Christian, then let the world see your heart.

Your future is full of big stages, and audiences await you out in this world. But do not ever lose sight of why you are here and who placed your gifts within you and gave you feet for dancing. God loves you, and God loves to be glorified. God didn't wait until you were old to give you salvation, so why should you wait until you are old to give Him glory?

The world is a dark place, and if God's children don't get out there and shed a little light in it, nobody ever will. One piece of advice that revolutionized my thinking was: "Your job doesn't have to be holy, but you must always be holy in your job."

Often in college I have gotten a lot of flak about being a journalism major. Many people think Christians have no place in the "evil media." But I disagree. After all, if Christians don't get out there, the news will become even more jaded and liberally biased. Or what about Hollywood? If Christians don't write good films and play good parts, then the world may never again see a truly good film. According to our Lord and Savior Jesus Christ, Christians are to be in the world but not of it. That gives you quite a bit of freedom when it comes to deciding on what you want to do with your life.

෨ ෨ ෨

High School and college are two of the most stressful times in your life. Everyone will ask you what you want to do with the rest of your life, and everyone will have a suggestion for you. "Go to USC. I'm an alum and it's a great school," or "I really think you should become a doctor; it's really the only honorable profession left these days," or similar words of advice will start to invade family gatherings as you get older. But in the long run, what you decide to do with your life is really between you and God.

On Thursday nights I am involved in a home Bible study, and we trade off the responsibility of leading each week. Recently my friend Sarah led it. We were going through Ephesians, and her passage was the last half of chapter three. She zoned in on verse 20 which says, "Now to Him who is able to do exceedingly abundantly above all that we ask or think, according to the power that works in us" (NKJV).

After she read it, she had all of us share our dreams and desires that we are normally afraid to share because they sound so unattainable. Each one of us started off by saying, "I know this sounds really stupid, but. . ." But in all honesty, nothing anyone said that night sounded stupid. One friend spoke of wanting to go into politics, another of wanting to go into entertainment, one of wanting to work with inner-city youth; one wanted to go into business with a prestigious company, and others wanted to be teachers and impact the lives of children in public schools. All these professions desperately need Christians.

I'll never forget what happened next. We were all talking about how nice it would be if those things could actually happen. I guess we must have had defeat in our voices or something because the next thing we knew, Sarah said, "Guys, why can't we do these things? After all, we are the ones with the exceedingly abundantly above!"

That shut us up real fast.

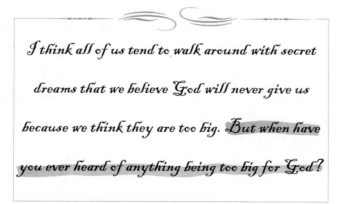

I think all of us tend to walk around with secret dreams that we believe God will never give us because we think they are too big. But when have you ever heard of anything being too big for God?

Don't you think He wants His children out there in all areas of life bringing people to Him through the things that they say and the way they live? I do.

⤚ ⤚ ⤚

Each of us is here on earth for a purpose, and we have received our dreams for a purpose. Perhaps you have short-term dreams like playing on a school sports team with many non-Christians. Perhaps you have long-term dreams like wanting to run for Congress and influence public policy. Or maybe your goal right now is just to survive at a public school. Dream big, trust God, and with His help you will succeed. We live in a world that says, "Believe in yourself." Christians need to get up on the world's stage and loudly proclaim, "I am here because I believe in God." Wherever you go and whatever you do remember God brought you there—and He has a purpose in mind for every step of your dance.

God even delights in doing the impossible. My friend Sam smuggled Bibles into China one summer. Everyone else in the customs line had his or her bag searched but Sam. I believe God kept the guards from searching her bag and seizing the Bibles. I had other friends, when they were college students, take the gospel to Cuba for the first time in the history of our school.

I think we often forget about that Ephesians 3:20 power that is at work within us.I think we forget that the Daniels and Davids of the Bible were called at a young age. We tend to forget that one man named Abraham became a father of many nations, and one man named Moses delivered an entire nation out of slavery. We think of Noah as a man we learned about in Sunday school, but we fail to remember that if he hadn't obeyed God and built the ark, life would have been wiped out in the Flood.

> *There is no limit to what God can do in and through you if you will let Him. Believe in God and what He can do.*

When Jesus came to earth and chose His twelve disciples, He didn't look in palaces, and He didn't hunt down the most beautiful people He could find. Instead He chose twelve ordinary men to live extraordinary lives. He even chose one who He knew wouldn't live up to the task.

When God saw that it was time to send His Son to the world, He put Him in the womb of an average teenage virgin. If Mary lived today, she could have been like you or one of your friends. What set Mary apart was the call that God had on her life. When she rose to meet that call, heaven applauded, for a star had finally started to shine.

> *When you rise to meet the tasks that the King of Kings has ordained for you, heaven erupts in thunderous applause. And the angels of heaven rejoice with God as He says, "That's my little girl. I always knew she could do it."*

And so it is with you. Your call sets you apart from others.

My friend Sherry's four-year-old daughter, Markie, will perform in her first dance recital tomorrow night. I asked my mom if Sherry was excited, and my mom laughed and answered, "Yes, but I think she's more afraid that Markie is going to get stage fright."

How many times does God our proud Father look down from heaven and see our stage fright? How many times do we push away His words of encouragement in Isaiah 41:10, " 'Do not fear, for I am with you; do not anxiously look about you, for I am your God. I will strengthen you, surely I will help you, surely I will uphold you with My righteous right hand.' "

Doing great things for God will not always be easy, but it will always be worth it. Biola University has a student-run missionary union on campus, which sends hundreds of students throughout the world with the gospel each year. Each trip is student led, student organized, and all of the fundraising is done by students. Since the 1920s, the university has sent countless students out each year because God keeps giving visions to new generations year after year.

We never need to fear the call when

we know who is calling us.

Through this program, so many of my friends are doing great things in missions. Other Christians I know have stellar voices and musical abilities and have landed record deals. I have friends who brighten the afternoon for elderly people in retirement homes every Friday. Some of my friends spend one night a week volunteering in after-school programs in the inner city, and I have friends who regularly visit patients in an AIDS hospice. These are all people who do great things for God every day. Although most of them go unnoticed by the masses, they are touching individuals.

Doing great things is not easy. Not only do we not get noticed for a lot of the things we do, we will also face challenges in the process. Just because you are called doesn't mean opposition will not arise. Whenever you dance, you will face critics, but in the end their reviews don't matter. As long as you are dancing for God, your work is being applauded. The Director of the whole show is smiling. Even though you may not see Him, you can be confident that He is there.

Whatever your gift, you are a star. God has cast you as the lead in the story of your life.

> *There are people to be touched and many who need to be reached. And you are the one God has chosen for the task.*

You may feel alone, and you may be scared. But God will never call you to do something without giving you the ability and the strength to do it.

One of the biggest events we've faced is 9/11. During spring break the following year, twenty-three of us from my college traveled from California to New York to help serve food to the workers at "ground zero." By the end of our week, everyone there knew who we were because they all thought college students should be spending their spring break in Cancun getting drunk. Instead, a handful of us went to share Christ in one of the areas where He was needed most. Our impact may have been small, but all of us on my team feel that in some way we touched history and history touched us as we shared the gospel in such a pivotal time. Weeks after we returned, my friend Leah said, "We are still at ground zero." She was right. The people's memories of our group coming to help them continued to make an impact on them that we would hear about later.

> *In many senses, all of us are still at work*
>
> *in the lives of those we haven't seen*
>
> *in quite some time.*

We don't always get to see the victories that will come as a result of our lives.

No matter what you are doing, somebody is watching your every move. You have the opportunity to touch that person in a way that nobody else can. You possess a powerful gift God has given you so that others will come to Christ. And when you mix that gift with the fruits of the Spirit (love, joy, peace, patience, kindness, goodness, gentleness, faithfulness, and self-control), then your dance will become divine.

There is no limit to what you can do if you let God guide your steps. It's been a long time since the world has seen a David or a Daniel or even a Moses.

> *It's time that you emerge from the shadows. Enough with the dress rehearsals and pipe dreams—it's time to dance.*

The stage has been set; the audience is in place. It's time to move them with the rhythm of your steps. It's time to shine. The Audience of all audiences is on His throne, and heaven is silently waiting for you to take the stage. And when you finally do appear, it will not matter what the world says because the applause of heaven will be ringing in your ears.

God is knocking on your dressing room door asking, "Is the dancer ready?" The answer is up to you.

Chapter 9

Rejoicing over Prodigals:
Dancing in Redemption

You may feel as if these pages display a fairy tale or a story you cannot attain. Perhaps you feel you have danced out of step too many times. Maybe you feel you're a failure because you've danced on the wrong stages and worn the wrong costumes. You may even feel as if you have given your all and have nothing left to dance with. But you're wrong.

If you are not feeling loved by God right now, it's because you are not letting Him love you.

The Divine Dance is a story of redemption more than anything else. It's a story written for girls and women wearing stained leotards and sporting tearstained faces. It's a story of grace for the sinner and of love being found again. You are a princess, and God has lavished His unconditional love on you.

He is desperately calling your name and begging you to come home. It does not matter how far you feel from heaven right now; you're only a heart's cry from the Master's love. You are only moments away from being whisked off into the dance of a lifetime. You may be standing on the outskirts of the dance floor, but God is extending His hand to you, and He is asking you to dance with Him.

Heaven is not just for people raised in Christian homes; it's not just for virgins or for those who have abstained from drugs and alcohol. Heaven is for anyone who will believe in the Lord Jesus Christ. Heaven is for you, but it is also for the worst person you know, if he or she chooses to accept it.

Whether you feel dirty or clean, no matter if you have wandered way off track or you have simply just begun to dance awry, God is still calling you home. Even if you have never danced with Jesus, He has crowned you queen of the ball and wants you to be His bride.

We view the Bible as a formal Book, and we fail to recognize that its story is timeless. Many who have heard and known the gospel from a young age miss its message for their own lives.

> *Jesus Christ is a captivating Lover,*
>
> *and sometimes we tend to lose sight of that.*

Perhaps you have wandered off course, and you still aren't sure how you fit into the Divine Dance. Maybe a million questions are running through your mind, or maybe you are haunted by your past sins.

> *Put all of that aside for one minute and let yourself be filled by one thought:*
>
> *God loves you. He always has, and He always will.*

Jesus Christ is the Son of God, and He died for the sins of this world. He rose again on the third day so we can all go to heaven to be with Him forever. . .yeah, yeah, yeah. We've all heard it before. And our hearts have grown hard to that story. We have forgotten what it is like to be lost and without God, or perhaps some of us have never known what it is like to live in a world where God does not exist. Others of us may feel too caught up in dark lifestyles for the light to even be able to shine on our lives. So let me invite you into a story. Follow me into the crowded theater and take a seat. The lights are dimming, and the dance is beginning.

Jesus is cast as the Lover. He is the hero with the white horse and everything else women dream of. A young girl hides from Him in the background. She is ashamed of her revealing dress and the suitcase full of emotional baggage she can't get rid of. Yet this hero who has all He could ever want is restless as He looks around. Something is still missing in His eyes. He knows and understands perfect love, but it is not enough for Him to share it with His Father alone. He faces a battle to win and a lover to woo, and Jesus is unsatisfied. He is waiting for someone. . . . He is waiting for you.

⌐ ⌐ ⌐

Just as you began this story as the little girl dancing on the stage begging your audience to adore you, you are now the young woman being sought by the Lover of all lovers. You are the one God is pursuing. Jesus Christ is standing in the middle of the dance floor, beckoning you to come to Him. Forget the fact that you are unworthy; forget the fact that you feel unloved and far from beautiful. Forget the mistakes you have made and the thoughts you have had. Abandon those things and run to the center of the dance floor and embrace your Lover. You have no need to hide from God.

He formed you in the womb, and He knows you well. Heaven wasn't home without you, so He came down to earth calling your name.

It's the story of a Lover who gave His life to be with you. In the time that Jesus was on earth, He gave up heaven for your heart. Are you withholding His greatest treasure from Him? You make God smile. Just the thought of you puts a song in His heart. And whenever you let Him hold you, He cannot help but dance.

> *The story of the Cross is a story of God loving mankind, but it is also the story of God loving you, as an individual.*

Like a child, you put your hands in His hands and your feet on His feet as you sway to the music and try to learn the steps. But it is as a lover that you lay your head on His shoulder as He holds you close. Perhaps this closeness happens only in God's dreams because you are living only in the shadows of a romance that could light this whole world on fire with its heat.

> *Perhaps you have never known God's passion,*
>
> *or maybe you have simply let it escape you.*
>
> *Either way, it's time to learn what love is all*
>
> *about and to start moving with the music.*

You have sat on the sidelines far too long. You have danced with too many unworthy lovers, and now it is time to dance with God.

The Book of Luke tells us of a man who had this type of experience. Most of us call him the prodigal son. Luke 15:11–32 tells us he had the world in his hands. Yet he asked his father for his share of the inheritance, and he packed his bags and left home. He squandered his money, partied it up, and searched for happiness. But he found, as we all eventually do, that this world is full of counterfeits, and real love cannot be found outside of God. As the young man was wallowing in pig slop, he came to his senses and returned home. And his father, resembling God Himself, ran to greet his son while he was still far away from home. He pulled out his finest robe, and he killed the fatted calf. There was music and dancing. The father rejoiced because his lost child had come home. That is how God views the return of His own prodigal children.

Maybe you read that story, and you feel more like the older brother who never left home and never dishonored his father. But why not celebrate with the prodigals when they return home?

Don't miss the dance because you have never left home. Grab your sisters and brothers who have returned, and dance until the sun comes up. Be thankful that you didn't have to endure the pigpens, but never condemn those who have. God loves all of His children equally, and He pursues all of us with the same vigor. Some of us are just harder to win over. Remember why you started dancing in the first place—because of God's love.

Those of us who have known God's love for a lifetime should be more than willing to dance with those who are just now learning of God's love and compassion.

Earlier in Luke 15, Jesus gave an analogy to the Pharisees and scribes who were always quick to judge Him. In Luke 15:4–7, He says: " 'What man among you, if he has a hundred sheep and has lost one of them, does not leave the ninety-nine in the open pasture, and go after the one which is lost, until he finds it? And when he has found it, he lays it on his shoulders, rejoicing. And when he comes home, he calls together his friends and his neighbors, saying to them, "Rejoice with me, for I have found my sheep which was lost!" I tell you that in the same way, there will be more joy in heaven over one sinner who repents, than over ninety-nine righteous persons who need no repentance.' "

God created you to love Him, and He has spent your entire life seeking you out and trying to convince you of that. He has saved you by grace and loved you with an everlasting love. But you have to accept that and believe that before you can be whisked away in the romantic dance that is known only by a woman who is loved for who she is.

> *But we are never unloved by God—*
>
> *even in the darkest alleys or the dirtiest*
>
> *crevices of our lives.*

You may feel completely unlovable. All of us do at one point or another.

Yes, God will bring light with Him when He enters our hearts, and we will be forced to give up our darkness to dance with Him. But He *never* stops loving us—not even for a minute. He comes to us as we are, and He scoops us up in His arms and carries us over a threshold into a new and vibrant life. God will put a ring on your finger and a song in your heart. His love lasts forever and knows no bounds.

> *Even in the middle of our affairs with the world,*
>
> *God still loves us and calls us His own.*

God knows your weaknesses; He knows your heartaches and your fears; He even knows everything you hide from the rest of world. He knows when you are pretending to dance, and He knows when you really are dancing. He knows when your heart is in it and when it is not. He knows when your heart is His, and He knows when it is divided.

And that is why we need Him. God made us weak so that in Him we can be strong.

The God who calls your name is the same God who made you for His pleasure. His heart will fill the needs of your heart, and He will make you whole. He will bind the wounds you bring to the ballroom, and He will clean the messes you have left in your wake. He will forgive and forget, and He will clothe you in robes of righteousness and royalty.

> *Satan wants you to feel as if you have been marked with the curse of the unlovely, but that is a lie. Beauty is in the eye of the beholder, and the One who is beholding you has tailor-made you to His liking.*

On a day when I was feeling particularly low, I received a note from my friend Erin. Its message stopped me in my tracks and lifted my spirits for a week. It said: "You are a child of the living God, the King of Kings and the Lord of Lords. You have the right to call the God of creation 'Daddy.' You have royal blood pumping through your veins. You are a princess in every sense of the word. As a child of the King, you have nothing to be ashamed of. Hold your head up high. Think like a princess. Speak like a princess. Act like a princess. Your Daddy is the King."

You, my friend, have royal blood in your veins. You are a princess. You have nothing to be ashamed of. Hold that head up and smile. God is smiling at you. Dance like nobody is watching but God, and forget about your past, forget about the present, and don't worry about the future.

> *You are destined for greatness,*
>
> *although it may be a different kind of*
>
> *greatness than you have ever dreamed of.*

God has a special purpose mapped out for your life, and no matter what you have done to mess it up, you have not succeeded. God's plan still stands, and if you let Him, He will complete the work He has begun in you.

There is always room to grow. All of us could afford to be a lot more like Jesus. We are all works in progress, but that is where the adventure comes in. You are young and have a lot of life ahead. Just think about what God could do through you if you are committed entirely to Him. Think about the passion God has given you. Be it art, writing, dancing, sports, or anything else, God made you good at it so you can give Him glory. Stop hogging the stage; stop having your pity party. Life is not about you anyway. It's about God.

So start dancing. Don't worry if people give you a hard time when you make the changes that come with turning your life around. Set firm boundaries for yourself, and avoid the things that have led you astray in the past. Break Satan's foothold as you flee temptation and embrace your King. God has cleared a place just for you in this performance, and it is your time to dance. In fact, it is time for you to dance like you have never danced before.

Ecclesiastes 3:4 says there is "a time to mourn and a time to dance." Your time of mourning your past and bearing its burdens has passed. If you have repented, God has moved on, and so should you. If you haven't repented yet, do so right now. Perhaps you have committed sexual sin, or maybe you just have a dirty mouth. Maybe you lie, cheat, or steal. Or maybe the pains of your past aren't even your fault. Perhaps you have been a victim of abuse or rape—those things, and others like them, are *not* your fault, and they *do not* make you dirty or tarnished in God's sight. He wants to free you from the pain of those things and release you from the ties that bind you to this world.

In repentance and forgiveness we find our redemption. In God's arms you will find freedom from all that has haunted you. And at the throne of grace, you will find acceptance for all that you are and all that you have the potential to become.

God is waiting. He wants to throw a welcome-home party in your honor. It doesn't matter if you have never set foot in church or if you have gone to church your entire life. If your heart is far from home and you want to know God like you have never known Him before, take off your mask and look up into the face of the One who calls you beloved.

Hold your head up high. Think like a princess, speak like a princess, act like a princess, and most importantly, dance like the princess you are.

An Audience of One:
Dancing with Delight

Often, by the time we get through the tangles of dancing with Christians, refusing to dance with non-Christians, honoring our parents, and using wisdom in dating, we are exhausted and realize we are dancing not out of passion but out of habit.

This was especially true for me at the beginning of my third year of college. My passion for God had dulled, but I didn't realize it until a Christian speaker came to our campus-wide Bible conference. " 'But I have this against you, that you have left your first love. Remember therefore from where you have fallen, and repent and do the deeds you did at first,' " the speaker said, quoting Revelation 2:4–5. I don't remember another word he said. I was too dumbfounded by the reality of my lukewarm passion for God.

There I sat with holes in my dancing shoes from all of the things I was doing for God. I had a head full of the finest biblical knowledge, and I was only three semesters away from having a minor in biblical studies.

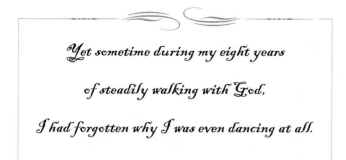

Yet sometime during my eight years

of steadily walking with God,

I had forgotten why I was even dancing at all.

Yes, I still loved God, but not like I did in the beginning. I was like an old bride who had gotten so caught up in her role as wife that she forgot why she married her husband. The love was still there, but the romance was gone. And for the life of me, I could not pinpoint when I had lost it.

The next day I left the Bible conference to spend a long weekend at my parents' house. I lay awake in my old bed trying to see where I went wrong. No answer came. But the next morning in solitude with God, things became a little clearer to me.

I had stopped getting excited about hearing His voice, and I'd stopped taking nuggets of Scripture as His personal words to me. Somewhere along the line, I forgot to make time for my private life with God. Yes, I was on the stage dancing my heart out, but I wasn't spending much time just sitting at His feet. My love for God was only a shadow of what it had once been.

> *Over time, I had gotten so busy dancing for God that I had forgotten to dance with God.*

I remembered a lesson I had learned the previous summer. Sometime before she died, my grandmother had packed away a box of mementos she wanted all of us to have when she was gone. So when we gathered at her house the day before the funeral, my family and I sat together and sorted through the box of heirlooms. One item caught all of us, including my grandfather, by surprise. Tied together with a thin pink ribbon was a stack of envelopes containing all of the love letters my grandpa had written her while he was in the navy.

On those carefully preserved pages were some of the most romantic words I had ever read, yet I had never seen that romantic element of my grandparents' relationship. "I wish I had known she saved these," my grandpa told us. "I would have read them to her in the last days of her life."

It was weird to think of my grandparents as being young and in love. I had always thought of them as, well, just grandparents. But they had a romance that was forgotten sometime through the years. Oh, don't get me wrong; the love was there, but there wasn't any of the gushy stuff that was in those letters.

And that was what had happened in my spiritual life. Years of studying the Bible had somewhat dulled its message to me. It had become too easy to view the Bible as I did my Spanish book or a textbook for one of my journalism classes. Sure, I still had quiet time alone with God in the mornings, but it was hurried and routine. I rarely left that time radiant from having been in God's presence. Sometime in between Bible classes, chapel, church, and home Bible study, I had become what I never wanted to be: a mediocre Christian.

Perhaps that is also where you are right now. Maybe years of church and ministry have stolen your fire, or maybe you have lived your whole Christian life in mediocrity. I've been in both places. I got saved at four years old, yet I didn't truly walk with God until I was thirteen. Being in a loveless relationship with God is the worst thing you can ever do because God is the designer of love; He is the Author of relationships, and He is the only One who will love you just as you are.

☙ ☙ ☙

It's time to go back to the analogy at the beginning of this book. You know the scene well by now. You are on the stage in your pink princess costume dancing away, but this time you have mastered the dance. The auditorium is empty except for the One who has been seated there all along. Even your balcony people have gone home for the night, and the entire world is fast asleep. You realize that you, too, are tired as you look into the face of the One who calls you beloved. He is smiling at you—no, He is beaming at you.

> *His eyes are dancing with delight as He watches you pour your heart out to Him.*

But He finally says to you, "Stop. You can come and rest awhile now."

You try to stop, but your feet keep moving. You're like the woman named Martha in Luke 10. This Scripture tells the story of Jesus visiting the home of two sisters and their brother. One sister, Martha, was busy preparing food for Jesus and the others who were there. But Mary, the other sister, just sat at Jesus' feet listening to Him, instead of helping her sister. Martha got upset that her sister wasn't helping, and she asked Jesus to tell Mary to get busy. Instead, Jesus pointed out that Martha needed to focus a little more on learning to relax with Him, just as Mary had done.

Like Martha, perhaps you don't know the song of Mary who sat at Jesus' feet just basking in His presence. Instead of spending time with Him, you focus your energies on performing for Him. Finally, in exhaustion you collapse and the stage goes dark. You cannot see a thing, but you hear footsteps approaching. Then a soft song surrounds the stage, and the Lover of your soul lights the room with His glory. He scoops you up into His arms and says, "I am so proud of you." As He brushes your hair out of your face, you can see that He is looking at you with both pride and adoration. His smile is contagious, and you are filled with joy. You begin to giggle with delight, and then you feel the wind in your hair. You realize you are dancing again, but this time God is dancing with you. The two of you are making spontaneous zigzags all over the stage. The faster God goes, the harder you laugh—you are having the time of your life. It's the world's best prom times a thousand.

The whole auditorium is filled with the music of life—your life. You could ask God anything in this moment, and He would tell you. Right now you two are the only ones in the entire universe. In this moment your soul is completely occupied with God alone, and worship and adoration flow freely from you.

When was the last time you felt like that? Just as in the beginning of the story, when you were too busy dancing for men and princes to notice the King, you have now become so enthralled with dancing for Him that you have forgotten the joy of feeling His touch. You have read the Bible, His love letter to you, like a textbook—if you have even read it at all lately. You have heard God's applause, but you have forgotten what it feels like to feel His pleasure. You have been dancing out of habit, and you have forgotten what it means to delight yourself in the Lord.

Psalm 37:4 says, "Delight yourself in the LORD; and He will give you the desires of your heart." So what does it mean to delight yourself in the Lord? I used to think that meant dancing for God alone and putting your all into the performance. But I've learned it means even more than that. It means to dance *with* God even more than you dance *for* Him. It means never letting the passions God has given you for other areas of life replace your passion for God Himself. It means getting so caught up in loving God that all of your desires are fulfilled in Him. How do you do this? You make time for God.

⤚ ⤚ ⤚

Place God as the number one priority in your life. At the risk of sounding cliché, this means putting Him on the throne, the reigning place, of your heart—which is usually quite easy when we first start a relationship with Him. But as time goes on, it is easy to get busy with other things. Luke 10:38–42 tells us that busyness has warred against worship for thousands of years. Most of us are the Marthas who are busy dancing *for* God, while there is a shortage of Marys who spend their days dancing *with* God.

God is easily taken off the throne of our hearts, because we allow other things into the throne room—the innermost chambers of our hearts. The easiest way to guarantee that God always remains on the throne of your heart is to seal the doors to the throne room shut. Do not let anything else near God's place in your heart.

Nobody and nothing ever need to be invited into that sacred place. Acknowledge that the place where God dances, and where you dance with Him, is holy ground. Refuse to let anyone else into your secret place with God—even other Christians. Don't ever let yourself have a fling with this world (or anyone else) on God's stage. Remember that we dance for a kingdom not of this world.

The throne room needs to be your special place for God. It needs to be your prayer closet where you go to get alone with God—the place where you can freely pour your heart out to Him and He can freely pour His heart out to you. It needs to be your personal ballroom where you and God can dance together to all of the high and low notes of life, as well as the great romance room where your flickering flame can go to become strong again. And most importantly, the throne room of your heart needs to be God's home. It does not need to be intruded upon by the short-stay guests who come and go in our lives. It needs only to be visited by you and God. So let your visits there be frequent and long.

≈ ≈ ≈

If you guard your relationship with God, nothing will ever be able to pose a threat to the passion of your romance.

> *Making God Lord of your life is a conscious choice you have to make every day.*

Just because you walked with God yesterday does not mean you will do it again today. We live in a world full of many worthless lovers. Cheap imitations will always be in vast supply. The world will vie for your attention until the day you die, and the temptation to dance for them once again will follow you all of your life.

The Divine Dance can't be fully understood from reading one little book. It can't be mastered in one day or one month or even one year—perhaps not even in one lifetime. But the Divine Dance is the story of the Christian life. It gives us purpose, it channels our passions, and it puts us in touch with God. It is what we were made to do. The speaker who told me I had left my first love offered me a solution. "Sometimes God gives us things that we love and that we love to do so we may grow to love Him more," he said.

And that is what the Divine Dance does. When we use our gifts and our passions to glorify God, when we stop performing for this world and start worshiping God, we grow to love Him more.

Those frustrating moments in God's studio pay off when you hit His stage, you do your best, and you make God smile.

Our individual moments with God in this dance are worth more than a million moments on the world's stage without Him.

The surprise wrapped up in the Divine Dance is that God wants to give each of us more than we could ever imagine. His plan for your life is far greater than anything you could ever dare to dream for yourself. Isaiah 55:8–9 says, " 'For My thoughts are not your thoughts, nor are your ways My ways,' declares the LORD. 'For as the heavens are higher than the earth, so are My ways higher than your ways and My thoughts than your thoughts.' "

The dance of romance is found in surrender. It is impossible to say the words "No, Lord." If you say no to God, you are not letting Him be Lord of your life. I don't understand why it is so hard for all of us who spend our lives trying to please our audiences to surrender to pleasing the most important Audience of all.

As disciples, we need to be like our Master. In the Bible we see that at various times Jesus retreated to be alone with God. He left people, ministry, friends, and family to spend time alone with His Father. Each of us needs to step off of the stage and spend time with God, too. We need to remember that we dance because we love God. When we dance for Him, He receives all of the glory He deserves. And when we make time for Him, He receives all of the love He deserves, as well.

We always need to keep our reason for dancing in the front of our minds. When we start to slip into old routines or we find ourselves dancing out of habit, we need to remember that it was God who created us to dance in the first place.

Each of us needs to spend our lives clinging to God, seeking to please Him, and desiring to know Him more. And if ever we begin to lose our focus, it's time to leave the stage and retreat to the throne room.

> *We need to let the information from the first nine chapters of this book direct our steps as we dance, but we need to let the message in this last chapter be burned into our hearts forever.*

Sometimes being on our knees isn't enough to make it in this life—we need to be on our faces before God. We need to praise Him, love Him, and honor and glorify Him in all that we do.

We must also remember that this dance is not a contest. Our worth is not determined from our steps—our worth was already determined a long time ago by the Choreographer. In God's eyes you are priceless. In God's eyes you are beautiful. In God's eyes you have a purpose, and He will do whatever He can to help you fulfill it. If that means letting you break your leg in cracks and crevices so you will realize you are dancing on the wrong stage, He'll do it. The key to dancing well is to listen to your Coach.

God is calling to you. Have you been listening? God is holding His arms out to you. Have you fallen into them? God has been wooing you since the day you were born. Have you ever even given Him the time of day? God made you His top priority when He sent Jesus to die in your place. Have you made Him number one in your life?

Life is full of steps and stages, costumes and characters, short notes and long pauses, and all of those things are orchestrated by the One who not only knows your name but also knows your heart. He has set your heartbeat to the rhythm of a certain song, and it is yours alone to dance to. And when you finally set your heart to do His will, and you begin to dance the Divine Dance, you will find that you are delighting yourself in the Lord, and all of the desires of your young heart will be fulfilled.

Dare to dream. Dare to hope. Dare to dance. Dare to fully be a daughter of the King of Kings. Put on your pink princess costume and make God proud. Dismiss the crowd one by one, and practice the majestic song of "God and I, God and I" that only comes from being alone with the Father.

I hope you dance!

> *When you dance with God,*
>
> *He will do things both in and through*
>
> *you that you never thought you could do.*
>
> *He will do things He isn't doing in and*
>
> *through anyone else. And when you dance for*
>
> *Him alone, He will clap louder than any*
>
> *audience you have ever heard.*

About the Author

Shannon Kubiak is a journalism major at Biola University in La Mirada, California. She has served as staff writer and copy editor for the *Biola Chimes* and won the *North County Times* "Excellence in Writing" award in 2000. She also speaks regularly to teen girls at retreats and conferences in southern California. She makes her home in San Diego. For more information, please visit www.shannonkubiak.com.